Get in the Sea!

Get in the Sea!

An Apoplectic Guide to Modern Life

ANDY DAWSON

MICHAEL JOSEPH
an imprint of
PENGUIN BOOKS

MICHAEL JOSEPH

UK | USA | Canada | Ireland | Australia
India | New Zealand | South Africa

Michael Joseph is part of the Penguin Random House group of companies
whose addresses can be found at global.penguinrandomhouse.com.

First published 2016

001

Copyright © Andy Dawson, 2016

The moral right of the author has been asserted

Set in 13.5/16 pt Garamond MT Std
Typeset by Jouve (UK), Milton Keynes
Printed in Great Britain by Clays Ltd, St Ives plc

A CIP catalogue record for this book is available from the British Library

ISBN: 978–0–718–18381–3

Contents

Introduction   vii

Society   I

Earth's Fifty Worst Humans: Part 1   46

Trends   59

Earth's Fifty Worst Humans: Part 2   90

Natural World   100

Sport and Leisure   114

Earth's Fifty Worst Humans: Part 3   136

Food and Drink   145

Hipster Shit   168

Earth's Fifty Worst Humans: Part 4   187

Miscellaneous Fuckery   195

Earth's Fifty Worst Humans: The Top Ten   228

Introduction

The sea. Dark, wet and, well . . . fucking enormous. Unforgiving, unknowable and a proper bastard to accurately weigh or measure, it is Planet Earth's soggy seductress, its damp temptress, its moist mistress. While parts of it are beautiful beyond all reason, most of the sea can only be described as 'a massive twat'.

Meanwhile, back on dry land, our day-to-day lives are being well and truly done up the wrong 'un by hordes of idiots who drag us down with their foolishness, their tompankery and their epic shithousery. Something must be done – it's time for the idiots to be dispatched into the fucking sea.

Take the United Kingdom, for example – a country governed over by a man who decided *not* to take legal action when his biographer claimed he had fucked a dead pig in the mouth when he was at university. Fucked it. In the mouth. With his cock. When it was dead. A pig. A dead pig. In the mouth.

Call me old-fashioned, but I reckon that's the sort of accusation you'd want straightened out once and for all in a court of law, in the full gaze of the people whose lives you are pretty much in control of. You want them to think you actually *did* face-bang a dead pig? That's your business, sunshine – but we now all know that the best place for you is languishing somewhere in the briny after being catapulted off the edge of a cliff.

For fuck's sake, we're hurtling towards 2020 – we were supposed to have evolved into a superior species by now. The daily grind of work was meant to have fucked off long ago, and we were explicitly told that we'd be living in sparsely furnished pods, watching hologram-based entertainment cavort and jig for us in the middle of said pod while we ate mashed potato served up by hysterical robots. Has it happened? Has it fuck.

Instead, those of us who can find a half-decent job are giving it fifty hours a week and then chucking our hard-earned coins at bearded halfwits in their cereal cafés, who are laughing like drains as they punt out bowls of Cheerios for three quid a go. Do we scoop up the halfwits and condemn them to the ocean? No – we just keep grinning and sucking up their soggy, milky offerings.

If we're not in thrall to the hipster cereal weirdos, we're insulting our ancestors and ourselves by paying through the nose for simple food that has been upscaled for us by toffs and fops. Obviously, the price has been upscaled as well, and you won't get much change from a tenner for the atrocity that is the artisan chip butty or a fish-finger sandwich that has inexplicably been tarted up with some kind of fucking leaf.

Thirsty after your overpriced breakfast twattery (which you'll probably have had at 5.30 p.m. because you're a bit ironic like that)? Just head for London's breathable cocktail cloud bar/art installation – it claims to be 'an alcoholic weather system for your tongue where meteorology and mixology collide'. Or, you know, dodge that shite along with its £12.50 entrance fee and just go to a pub instead. You know what isn't breathable? The fucking sea.

In fact, fuck that whole idea of a 'Leisure Age' – you were sold a lie. We're all hard workers now, or at least we are according to the Conservative government, which is keen to reward workers and chastise shirkers. It's the British way, right? Work until you drop.

Call me cynical and old-fashioned, but I've got a natural aversion to anyone who claims to prefer working to shirking. Some of us have got shirking down to a fine art – thirty-five-minute toilet breaks, a ready excuse whenever the boss needs someone to do a couple of extra hours at the end of the day in exchange for time off in lieu, and at least three grandparents' funerals to get time off for every single year.

Hard workers? Fuck 'em. Untrustworthy little arse-licking shitehawks. No one ever built an empire through hard work. You build an empire through taking the fucking piss. The hardest work you should find yourself doing will involve putting a gang of these suspicious, so-called hard workers in the fucking sea.

Is there a criterion for sea insertion, you might wonder. Is there a science to all of this? No, as you'll see as you read this book, the only people and things that will be put in the fucking sea will end up there solely because they deserve it.

The sea is for the shits, the pricks, the wankers, the twats, the fuckwads, the pisswheels, the goons, the fools, the tools and the cunts. The cunts, the cunts, the cunts; the complete and utter cunts.

Consider cunts such as private landlords – they're sleeping like logs each and every night in giant nests made from excess cash while their tenants endure rising damp, psychotic neighbours and leaking ceilings that drip asbestos-tainted water on to the foreheads of their children. Fuck that – get those landlords in the fucking sea.

Consider meggings – leggings, but marketed for men. You'll see them worn by men who are slightly too old to not realize that they're making an alarming error, as well as all-round shitheads. You'll see them and you'll wonder why their owners are not being harassed by crabs as they flail at the bottom of the fucking sea.

Consider an actual paint colour called 'Mole's Breath' and the audacity of its makers to charge £72 for a five-litre bucket of the stuff. Consider 'Brosé' – the recent cunt cult in which grown adult men gather together and slurp rosé wine. Consider UKIP, and 'banter', and YouTube stars who earn millions of quids for filming themselves gurning into an iPhone camera while they're playing Grand Theft Auto.

Consider an empty London garage being advertised as a 'studio flat' and going on the market for £117,000 while nearby half-starved people sleep under a bush. Consider legal highs and wonder why people can't just get the job done by sniffing glue any more. Consider twenty-four-hour rolling news cack, people who set up Twitter accounts for their own fucking cats and open-mic nights at comedy clubs, which should really come with a warning that you'll want to try and swallow your own eyeballs after forty seconds of the inept tripe that appears on stage.

All of that. All of that raging arseholery needs to get in the fucking sea. But that's just scratching the surface . . .

Society

Social media charity crazes

We're all united in the belief that raising money for a good cause is, on the whole, something to be applauded. The clue is in the phrase 'good cause' – if you were trying to raise cash for a bad cause, such as strapping old ladies into shopping trolleys and sending them careering down a hill into a bramble hedge, people would be less inclined to dig deep into their pockets.

The meteoric rise of social media has proved to be a huge shot in the arm for the charity scene. Once upon a long ago, the lads and lasses who want to ban cancer and stop child cruelty were forced to rattle tins in the street, but now their fundraising happens on the Twitter and the Facebook, and we all get to take part in wacky little stunts while we're about it.

Which is where the problems begin (and it was going *so* well). The stunts start to overtake the fundraising.

Remember the ice bucket challenge? Any idea which charity it was in aid of? Do you recall making a donation yourself?

No, of course not. But you were out there in your garden, weren't you, tipping a bucket of Baltic-temperature water over your head while one of your associates filmed it all on your phone. Up it went on to Facebook, you raked in the likes and shares and lolz, and because the challenge was the forfeit, you were under no obligation to donate. Well done, fucko.

I'll bet the tireless workers at WaterAid UK, who campaign for safer water supplies in underdeveloped countries, were pissing themselves laughing at the hundreds of thousands of gallons you were pouring all over your gardens and office car parks while not donating any money anywhere.

It didn't end there either – there was the No Make Up Selfie Challenge, where women went barefaced on Facebook in order to raise cash for . . . oh, fuck knows what it was. It's unknown how much cash was pledged, but there was definitely a vast haul of comments along the lines of 'Awwwww, hun you look GAWJUS!' and suchlike.

Then there's Movember – the one fundraising stunt that requires its participants to do *less* than they normally would, by growing a moustache across the course of a month. The added danger is that it leads to thousands of men wandering around looking like paedophiles, making it tougher to spot the real ones.

Perhaps the absolute nadir of it all was the 30 Day Squat Challenge For Nepal. Everyone wins with that one – the Nepalese people get a few quid to help rebuild their earthquake-decimated homes while the participant gets a really tight set of buns.

RAISING AWARENESS IS NO SUBSTITUTE FOR RAISING DOSH – IF YOU DON'T

CHUCK IN SOME CASH WHILE YOU'RE
PLASTERING YOUR OWN FACE ALL OVER
FACEBOOK, YOU NEED TO GET IN THE
FUCKING SEA.

Tattoos

If you've got any common sense whatsoever, you should
be investing in some tattoo removal equipment, training up a small army and renting business units in every
town and city across the land.

That's because there's a wind of change coming – at
some point over the next decade, there's going to be a
fuckload of people waking up to the fact that they've
lumbered themselves with shit tattoos.

Whether it's the name of your current partner
scrawled across the top of your shoulders or an entire
arm devoted to a scene showing the late Paul Walker
from the *Fast and Furious* movies behind the wheel of a
Porsche in heaven, there's been some serious errors of
judgement made by young people, and they're going
to be desperate to get their tattoos erased as they hit
their forties and they become the kind of sour-faced
old fucker who criticizes people who have tattoos in a
book.

WHEN YOU'RE SEVENTY-SEVEN, DO YOU
REALLY WANT A NURSE TO TAKE A
BLOOD SAMPLE FROM AN ARM THAT'S

GOT A POLYNESIAN PATTERN FROM TOP
TO BOTTOM? GET IN THE FUCKING SEA
AND SCRUB YOURSELVES CLEAN.

Shop doorway conversationalists

It's lovely to catch up with someone you haven't seen for
a while. You can fill each other in on your latest news –
Maureen's hip replacement; John's new job doing nights
in B&Q; the fact that your next-door neighbour is almost
certainly doing webcam shows – while keeping all of the
really grim stuff to yourself.

But when you bump into each other in the doorway
of a shop and make no attempt to retreat to a place that
is more convenient for everyone else around you, you're
no better than the ISIS terrorists that are threatening
the future safety of our beautiful planet.

See also the primary-school gate when you're dis-
patching your little darlings and before you head off for
Zumba and some secret 11 a.m. wine. And the impromptu
catch-up that takes place in the middle of a supermarket
aisle with a couple of trolleys strategically placed so that
no other fucker can get past them.

GET THE FUCK OUT OF THE FUCKING
WAY, YOU SELFISH PIG DOGS. MOVE
YOUR SLACK-JAWED GOSSIPING AWAY
FROM THE THOROUGHFARE OR GET IN
THE FUCKING SEA WITH IT – SOME OF

US ARE TRYING TO GET INTO FUCKING
CARD FACTORY.

Feet-on-seat train cunts

Perhaps we're doing society all wrong. Perhaps there
needs to be more citizen justice out there. Maybe if we
were all armed with stun guns linked up to some kind of
central HQ that would grant us authority to use them,
the world would be a better place.

No, stay with me on this one – here's how it works.
You get on a train and are sat across from some complete and utter wanker who has put his feet on the seat
opposite. This needs sorting.

You pull out your stun gun in readiness. Using an app
on your phone, you make contact with Social Justice
HQ, selecting 'feet on seat train cunt' from a list of
available transgressions. You can even slyly upload a
photo of the offender.

At HQ, someone looks at your submission and
grants you authority to proceed. Your stun gun is
remotely unlocked and you give the seat feet fuckwad a
quick blast of laser or electricity or however these things
work.

Slumped in his seat and now unconscious, you remove
his feet from the seat and go back to your business. Maybe
you leave a Post-it note on his forehead so that he knows
why he's been punished once he wakes up, preferably a
few miles after his intended station of alightment.

Will he learn? Hopefully – the world will be a better place, and you'll have played out your ongoing fantasy about doling out instant justice to anti-social mother-fuckers for real. Until then, we can but dream.

THIS IS THE FUTURE WE TRULY CRAVE, AS OPPOSED TO A FUTURE OF BLUE-TOOTH DOG-WALKING AND FUCKING TINDER. GET US TOOLED UP SO WE CAN ZAP THESE WANKERS OR EVEN PUT THEM ON A TRAIN BOUND FOR THE FUCKING SEA.

Dubai

'You simply must go to Dubai,' said an old friend recently, shortly before I wandered away, glassy-eyed at the tedium of it all. He babbled something about the hotels, the futuristic skyline, the decadence, the culture and the amazing social scene, but I zoned out and started thinking about my favourite bits from *The Simpsons* instead.

I can't be sure but I don't think he mentioned the reports that some of the 250,000 foreign labourers in the city have been alleged to live in conditions described by Human Rights Watch as being 'less than humane'.

He waxed lyrical about some grand horse race meeting that he'd been to, but I can't remember him saying anything about the reports of up to ten foreign construction workers living in the same room in what were basically labour camps, or the fact that many of them are trapped in a cycle of poverty and debt, which amounts to little more than indentured servitude.

But he had a lovely tan, so who was I to piss all over his parade?

IF YOU LIKE YOUR HOLIDAYS TO BE FOUNDED ON THE SWEAT AND BLOOD OF MODERN SLAVERY, YOU NEED TO GET IN THE FUCKING SEA. NOT A NICE SEA, LIKE IN DUBAI BUT THE NORTH SEA, NEAR ABERDEEN, IN FEBRUARY.

Racist marches in town centres

Now that football hooliganism seems to be a relic, condemned to the history books and two-bob films like the truly woeful *Green Street 3: Never Back Down*, there's a certain section of white, working-class blokes who need something to do on a Saturday afternoon. Something that will satiate their thirst for congregating in large groups, drinking low-strength lager and being a fucking massive pain in the arse for other citizens who are just trying to go about their business.

That's about as good a way as any to explain the rise of the BNP (which has since fallen again) and the EDL – the English Defence League, a pretend army for men who haven't got the minerals to serve in the actual army.

There's usually about a hundred of them and they turn up en masse in assorted towns around the land, all legitimate and pre-planned, so that the small traders in said towns can know in advance that their day's takings will be non-existent, edging them closer towards financial ruin.

If you think about it, it's a bit ironic that the major casualties from the demonstrations by these men who want to keep England 'pure' and the way it used to be are small, independent traders, the sort of people who run pet shops and motor spares stores, but perhaps that concept is a bit too deep for these fuckers to wrap their heads around.

The day always pans out the same – there's some wandering around, some chanting, some racism that tries to pretend it isn't racism, a mild skirmish with the local anti-fascist brigade, and then everyone goes home.

Absolutely fuck all is achieved, no minds are changed, England stays more or less exactly the same, and the small traders go home and plough into a bottle of cheap scotch.

DIVERT YOUR LUNK-HEADED, KNUCKLE-DRAGGING CUNT PARADES AWAY FROM OUR STRUGGLING TOWN CENTRES AND MAKE A BEELINE TOWARDS THE FUCK-ING SEA INSTEAD.

Fancying a holiday or maybe just a night out at a local restaurant but don't want to fuck it up and end up with tuberculosis, salmonella poisoning or a punch in the side of the head from a surly proprietor? TripAdvisor is the site for you!

Filled with reviews of everything from two-star all-inclusive hell holes in Magaluf to visitor farms where you can ride around on the back of Highland cattle, Trip-Advisor's major selling point is that its reviews are submitted by us, ordinary members of the public. '200m+ unbiased reviews', it claims in its blurb.

Couple of points here. I've spent a lot of time on Trip-Advisor over the years and I'm not sure where they get 'unbiased' from. There's definitely a contingent of reviewers on there who have raw bias pumping through their veins. Bias against the world and everything in it.

To say that some people on there are never satisfied is a thundering understatement. 'The bed in my room was overly firm, there was a smudge of what might have been ink on the hairdryer and the noise from some roadworks half a mile away at 7.38 a.m. drove me halfway insane before I had the lukewarm eggs in my all-you-can-eat breakfast.' Mate, you're just a miserable cunt, and no hotel stay is ever going to change that.

Secondly, there's the problem of reviews being

submitted by ordinary members of the public. Have you fucking *seen* the state of the public? Have you been out there recently? Jesus – they make your average low-budget zombie massacre film look like a cheerleader pageant. The last group of people any of us ever should be taking advice from is the general fucking public.

Thirdly, not only is TripAdvisor's vast knowledge bank of 'unbiased' reviews fashioned from the brains of the fucking public, it's by those members of society who (a) feel that their opinion is worth sharing with others, and (b) have the time and energy to do this. In other words, fucking psychos.

TripAdvisor, then – an enormous database of utter tripe written by mentalists. Enjoy!

LET'S SEE SOME OF THESE WANKERS SUBMIT A REVIEW ABOUT THEIR STAY AT THE BOTTOM OF THE FUCKING SEA.

Removing danger from children's lives

Childhood is a time of awe and wonder. When you're a kid, your brain is basically a sponge, soaking up knowledge and experience, processing it all, developing emotions and slowly transforming you into the adult you'll become.

Helpfully, that magical brain is protected by a hard skull, designed to stop you from dying instantly if you fall off your bike or out of a tree. The problem is that it rarely gets tested any more, because we're too concerned with eliminating all risk from kids' lives instead of letting them career down hills on go-karts or climb up electricity pylons to retrieve a stuck kite.

They're not even allowed to make a slide in the school playground when it's icy any more, and they make them wear crash helmets when they do spelling tests, and Snickers are banned from the lunch boxes in case someone with an allergy inhales a nut, and their parents have to sign a waiver form if the kids are going to come into contact with a plastic bag or other light suffocation hazard, and, and, and . . .

LOSING AN EYE AT AN EARLY AGE IS CHARACTER BUILDING AND THE SOFT ARSES WHO SUGGEST OTHERWISE NEED TO BE FIRED RIGHT INTO THE FUCK-ING SEA.

Milibollocks

Poor Ed Miliband – not only did he lose the 2015 general election to an unscrupulous gang of utter, *utter* shitheels, he was roundly humiliated into the process too. As well as being castigated by the cunts in the tabloids because his face turned into a wonky mask of rubberized weirdness when he chewed a bacon sandwich once, there was the rash of memes and mini Miliband cults that sprung up too.

Who among us doesn't feel a bit sick when they look back at Milifandom, where Ed was briefly transformed into some kind of teen idol among young female lefties? You can probably feel your genitalia shrinking in horror as you recall the Ed Stone, a chronically ill-advised piece of rock with Ed's electoral pledges carved into it.

It even carried on after the election, when he appeared in public sporting a rash of salt-and-pepper stubble – that, of course, was the Milibeard.

Here's one that will kill it all to death – 'The Human Milipede'. Just like the Human Centipede film, but with Ed and his brother David and clones of themselves. Hundreds of them. Mmmmm . . .

NOT SURE WHAT GOES IN THE FUCKING SEA HERE, BUT DON'T GET COMPLACENT BECAUSE HIS FUCKING BROTHER WILL BE BACK SOON TO STINK UP POLITICS AGAIN.

Buying a brand-new car

You see them on their driveways, those blokes polishing their gleaming new pride and joy, and you pity them. You also wonder if they've realized that their glimmering, purring new vehicle will be worth a mere fraction of what they've forked out in a year's time.

They probably don't care, though, because the

brand-new car helps to mask all those fears they live with day after day. You know, the fears about the size and performance of their dicks.

Rather than splash out on a brand-new car, simply buy a twelve-month-old one instead and fit a wood chipper on to the roof. Then, stuff a load of money into it and drive around, spewing a confetti of cash into the sky everywhere you go. It's the same thing.

YOUR SPOTLESS, GLEAMING, PURRING IDIOT MACHINE WILL BE WORTHLESS AFTER THE HANDBRAKE HAS BEEN LEFT OFF AND IT HAS BEEN GENTLY NUDGED TOWARDS THE CLIFF EDGE AND ITS WATERY FUCKING GRAVE.

Forced jollity

'And that's Michael over there – he's in charge of fun in the office.'

'In charge of . . . fun? What does that entail exactly?'

'Oh, you know – he organizes our nights out. Karaoke, murder mystery nights, vicars and tarts parties. He's mad, is Michael.'

'Ah. I see.'

'And when it's Red Nose Day, he organizes all the fundraising events – he wore a crown filled with milk last year! Crazy!'

'Hmmm . . . '

'He's responsible for so much office morale-boosting. Paper aeroplane Friday, hula hoop contests, dance-offs . . .'

SOMEONE OUGHT TO DO A MASSIVE VIOLENCE ON MICHAEL AND THEN DROP HIM IN THE FUCKING SEA.

Twee swearing

Swearing is an art form, for fuck's sake, and anyone who tells you it is a sign of a limited vocabulary and a stunted mindset can go and piss up a fucking rope. Sadly, even profanity is becoming infested with the abominable tweeness that is killing the twenty-first century before it's really got going.

Arseholes (and it's always arseholes) are taking the swearwords that we love and skilfully deploying and fluffing them up, thereby completely ruining them. I'm talking *cockwomble*, I'm talking *twatbadger*, I'm talking *shitwizard*, *cuntpuffin*, and I'm talking *fucktrumpet*.

There's *pissweasel*, *arsebiscuits* and *fucksocks* as well, but they aren't used quite as often, but we must remain vigilant. All in all, this shit needs to be ended ASAP – these are the kinds of words that you could imagine being used on CBeebies in a few years if we're not careful, and then the infantilizers will have won, and swearing will be lost to us for ever. Fuck that.

IF YOU'RE NOT GOING TO FUCKING SWEAR PROPERLY YOU NEED TO FUCKING GET IN THE FUCKING SEA.

Euthanasia deniers

Sure, you're sat there right now, reading this book and nodding your head sagely at its many, very correct views. One day, though, you won't be able to read. You'll barely be able to see, your hearing will be shot to shit, and the highlight of your day will be a bed bath or a colostomy bag change.

If you've got your wits about you by then (which you almost certainly won't have), you'll be praying for the sweet relief of death, which should be your right, surely?

Apparently not – we humans are still being told when we can and can't pop our clogs, even though Freddie Mercury set a stunning precedent over two decades ago by singing 'Who Wants To Live Forever?' and then snuffing it.

Who the fuck has the right to tell us that we have to stay alive and suffer unimaginable levels of pain if faced with some kind of horrific terminal illness? Why can't the money that will be spent on heroic doses of pain relief just be spent on a cocktail of drugs that will end it all before it gets too bad and mean that our loved ones don't have to watch us fall apart before their very eyes.

The Swiss have got their Dignitas clinic, and before long there'll be busloads of dying people heading there, exercising their right to end life how and when they choose to. We're grown-ups, for fuck's sake – we can handle it.

OR YOU COULD JUST GET IN THE FUCK-ING SEA – IT'S HARDLY IDEAL THOUGH.

Black Friday

Another unwelcome import from America, to go with school proms and the transformation of Halloween into a major industry from what used to be a bit of a mooch around the estate while brandishing a hollowed turnip with a candle in it.

On the day after Thanksgiving, Americans tradition-ally get out of bed at 3 a.m. and waddle off to the shops before fighting each other for cheap coffee machines and half-price laptops. The whole thing is an unedifying (yet lucrative) pre-Christmas shambles, so naturally we're embracing it with open arms in the UK.

The quality of the bargains that can be had is highly debatable, so the best course of action is to ignore the whole thing, sit back and wait for the viral videos to appear on the internet.

You know what I'm on about – some fucker bringing a 42" plasma TV screen down over the head of another fucker who has just tried to wrestle it from them. An Asda trolley with a crying toddler in it being used as a battering ram in order to scatter a crowd and get to a

£19 drill before anyone else does. People who would usually hold doors open for one another eye-gouging for a cut-price air fryer.

Get a grip, dickheads.

YOU WANKERS WOULD RUN HEADLONG INTO THE FUCKING SEA IF YOU THOUGHT THERE WAS A TEN-QUID SODA STREAM IN IT FOR YOU.

The Sunday Times *Rich List*

Ooooh, how intoxicating! A detailed rundown of a thousand people with loads more money and much better lives than the rest of us – and they're probably a total pack of bell ends as well.

You don't usually get turbo-rich by being kind and lovely and going around picking snails up off the pavement and moving them out of harm's way, so it's fair to assume that the Rich List is littered with brazen shitheels, genuine psychopaths and rotten old bastards.

Coincidentally, it's presented for your delectation in a newspaper owned by Rupert fucking Murdoch.

TAKE YOUR BILLIONS AND GET IN THE FUCKING SEA, WHERE YOU'VE PROB-ABLY ALL BUILT SECRET UNDERWATER HIDEAWAYS TO BE USED IN THE EVENT OF A NUCLEAR HOLOCAUST.

Manspreading

Fellas, it's been apparent for a long time that some of you are improbably proud of your meat and two veg – we know this because you spread your legs wide apart and put it on display, often on public transport. Perhaps you think it'll look even more endearing when it's all shuddering gently along with the vibrations of the train.

Pack it in, though, eh – you're making innocent people nauseous, and the chances of you getting laid as a result of your animalistic show of 'strength' is almost zero.

'Mmmmm . . . he's giving off some sexy vibes – I think I'd like to get me a ride on some of *that*,' said no woman to herself ever when faced with a manspreader.

CLOSE YOUR FUCKING LEGS, DICK-HEADS. THE WORLD DOESN'T NEED TO SEE YOUR PUTRID GENITALIA OR CATCH AN UNSOLICITED WHIFF OF YOUR PEN-ILE ODOUR. KEEP 'EM TOGETHER OR GET IN THE FUCKING SEA.

The bedroom tax

If there's a single piece of government legislation that is aimed at making ordinary, decent people feel like utter scum, it's the bedroom tax, as introduced by the coalition government as a great way to rake in a few extra quid, inconvenience the fuck out of huge swathes of the population and demonize the poor that little bit more.

How does it work? If you're claiming housing benefit, your payment will be restricted if you've got any spare bedrooms, and you can only claim for the bedrooms that you or your family are occupying. Which is super fucking cunty.

Kids away at university for three years and then planning to come home afterwards? Tough shit – you can't claim housing benefit for their empty room. Cough up, fucko.

Maybe you could take in a lodger? After all, there'll probably be lots of people who can't afford to rent a full house now that the bedroom tax is up and running – they could come and live with you.

Brilliant! Cram all the poor people into little houses together and then maybe the spare ones can be snapped up by private landlords! Fucking the poor is *easy*!

THE PACK OF CUNTS THAT CAME UP WITH THIS OBSCENITY OF A GOVERNMENT POLICY SHOULD BE ENTOMBED IN A BOX ROOM IN A COUNCIL FLAT IN THE MIDDLE OF THE MOST DOWNTRODDEN PART OF BRITAIN AND LEFT UNTIL THEY'RE REDUCED TO EATING EACH OTHER. THE SEA WOULD BE LIKE A FUCKING HOLIDAY CAMP BY COMPARISON.

The internet is arguably the greatest scientific leap forward since the steam kettle but, as with everything else in the entire world, it has been fucking ruined by humans.

At first, we thought that newspapers would be improved by going online. For one thing, they would be free, but they'd also be able to use more pictures and eventually, videos too. How very modern!

But what also came along was the comments section – a citadel of deranged evil that exists under the 'proper' stuff on every newspaper's web page (except for the ones that have wisely removed them altogether).

It's an infinite number of monkeys using an infinite number of keyboards to spout an infinite quantity of cyber-shite all over our beautiful internet. Any kind of prejudice you can imagine can be found there, along with some kinds that you didn't know existed and one or two that have been devised by their author just for the occasion.

Points are missed more often than they're made, and that's being kind about the lawless trollathon that thousands of wankers contribute to every hour of every day. The people whose job it is to moderate comments sections will all be making huge industrial injury claims for post-traumatic stress disorder in fifteen years' time.

Not so long ago, the twisted wrong 'uns responsible for most of the comments on websites would have instead scribbled their thoughts in green crayon to their local newspaper editor, who would have quite rightly saved them all up before incinerating them en masse at the office Christmas party.

If you've ever left a comment on a website, congratulations – you're directly responsible for making the entire world 17 per cent worse than it was before the internet was invented.

GET IN THE FUCKING SEA, YOU PURVEYORS OF THE BIGGEST CULTURAL ATROCITY SINCE THE NAZIS RAN OFF WITH ALL THAT ART.

The word 'mumpreneur'

Are you a bright spark with a winning business idea tucked up your sleeve, ready to unleash it upon the world? But are you also a woman who once had a tiny human tucked up her womb, which you have already unleashed and are now hoping to provide for with the help of your ring-a-ding business plan?

Sorry, but you can't be both – you must now be defined as a third kind of being – the mumpreneur. Spooning smooshed-up butternut squash into your infant's mouth with one hand while hammering out turnover projections for the next three years on a scientific calculator with the other.

Childcare is not an option – if you're not haggling

with Chinese suppliers with your Bluetooth headset while simultaneously pushing your toddler on a swing in the park, your life is totally invalid.

You're a mumpreneur now so you'd better get those business cards amended.

SURELY THE AGE OF THE 'SEAPRENEUR' IS ALMOST UPON US. ONLY ONE FUCK-ING WAY TO FIND OUT.

The word 'hipsterpreneur'

If you thought the mumpreneur was bad, think again because here's a word that will have you gagging and reaching for the nearest receptacle to be violently sick into.

Are you a bright spark with a winning business idea tucked up your sleeve, ready to unleash it upon the world? But are you also a cunt who goes around looking like a lumberjack, riding a unicycle and paying for an ice-cold coffee that's been flavoured with Turkish Delight and is served up in a café that's also a working abattoir as well as a £200-a-day drop-in centre for school-refusers?

You, you fucker, are a hipsterpreneur. Thankfully though, your business will be niche, short-lived and almost certainly ridiculous. An app that finds the nearest source of granola dust for example. Or an exclusive moustache oil that is blended with the stomach juices of a rare East Asian breed of capybara.

HIPSTERS. EVERYWHERE. WORSE THAN FUCKING EBOLA. PUT THEM ALL IN THE FUCKING SEA.

The 5p carrier bag crisis

In May 2015, England (yes, it was England that was to blame) casually elected a government that seems hell-bent on making life as tough as possible for the neediest members of society, stripping away their financial support and possibly condemning many to an early death.

Weirdly, the majority of us have blindly accepted this rank old state of affairs, choosing instead to focus our rage on the abolition of free carrier bags in supermarkets.

By October 2015, the English were up in arms at what some exceptional pricks were calling the 'bag tax'. No longer will they be able to fill that cupboard under the sink with tens of thin carrier bags, stuffed into each other and ignored like some giant ball of uselessness. It's five pence a pop now, so you'd better start recycling the ones you've got or invest in bags for life instead.

While Wales and Scotland have been calmly and quietly getting on with the bag tax since 2011, England reacted to it with the kind of self-absorbed shrieking that you'd expect.

Stories quickly appeared online about people being apprehended by supermarket security guards after they'd tried to swerve the 5p charge by taking their groceries home in a basket, escalating to others nicking the trolleys they'd been wheeling their shopping around in after getting through the checkout.

Imagine half-inching a shopping trolley and pushing £40 worth of groceries all the way home in it just so you could dodge forking out a few extra pence for the trusty, reliable carrier bags that you previously believed to be your birthright. And then putting a photo of what you'd done on fucking Facebook. Such pride. Such fuckery.

FEWER PLASTIC BAGS WILL HELP THE EARTH BREATHE AGAIN BUT YOU FUCKERS WILL NOT FEEL THE BENEFIT AS YOU WILL BE LANGUISHING IN THE FUCKING SEA.

Workers' rights

Starship might have supposedly 'built this city on rock and roll', but modern Britain was built on the relentless toil of generations of hard-working men and women. And that is how it should be – no matter how many people they had grafting for them, there's no way that Starship could have come up with Birmingham solely using rock and roll. But I digress.

For the past century or so, things have been pretty cushty for workers, with mass employment, unions standing up for them and looking out for their needs, and a distinct absence of abject poverty or any kind of plague. Well done, everyone!

Recently, though, that's all been fucked up beyond all recognition. What with Thatcher smashing the unions and killing off heavy industry, right through to subsequent governments passing laws that make your job as secure as a scarecrow in a hurricane, even if you've got a job, you're possibly just one small quirk of fate away from living in a ditch.

With zero-hours contracts in vogue, you might get a thirty-hour working week or it might just be three. Got a problem with that? Fuck off, pal – there's plenty of other people who are dying to pick items from this sportswear warehouse. Not literally dying, but then again . . .

Think you've been unfairly dismissed? Unless you've been in your job for two years, your case won't even get a hearing. And if it does, employment tribunal fees rocketed in 2013 (subsequently, claims fell by more than half), so do you really want to take the gamble?

It's dead simple – you belong to big business, and big business has its hand jammed down the trousers of government. You're a speck, an amoeba, a barely acknowledged statistic. So shut the fuck up and work through your dinner hour like your colleagues have started doing. You wouldn't want to upset your boss, would you?

MODERN SLAVERY NEEDS TO GET RIGHT IN THE FUCKING SEA.

Some of us have been aware of these two mighty inter-lopers on to the supermarket scene for years. Some of us get wriggly with anticipation when next week's special offers are about to be posted online. Some of us don't even mind standing in the checkout queue for ages because we know that the weirdly named German cake we've got in the trolley is going to be fucking delicious.

But it's getting tough in there. The broadsheet readers have woken up to the joy of cheap cycling gear, affordable power tools and bath mats that are 80 per cent less fluffy than ones in John Lewis but at only 15 per cent of the price.

They're wandering around in there like they're empire builders who have just stumbled upon a colony of jewel-rich brown-skinned folk that are ripe for plundering. It's gentrification at its most disgusting and it sometimes means I have to queue for my loose-sold pistachio nuts. Raging.

GET BACK TO YOUR FANCY PANTS WAIT-ROSE DREAMLAND OR GET IN THE FUCKING SEA.

The Christmas Coca-Cola truck

Coca-Cola must think they own Christmas – after all, it was they who put Santa Claus in a red suit for the very first time. Well, them or the Bishop of Myra back in the fourth century – the jury's still out on that one.

Either way, the festive period has somehow become inextricably linked with the purveyors of sugary pop, and the sound of their 'Holidays are coming' bullshit advert jingle means that Christmas has got you well and truly in its grip.

So hypnotic is it that the advert's truck is now almost as big a star as Santa, Jesus and all the other big names of the festive season. The truck goes on tour each December, turning up in assorted towns and cities, where people take leave of their senses and queue up to meet the fucker.

That's right – you can meet the truck and have your photo taken with it. A photo that you have a 1 per cent chance of looking at again at any future point in your life, and if you do, you'll feel something in between emptiness and revulsion.

HEY COCA-COLA – SANTA DOESN'T DRINK COKE, HE DRINKS RED BULL, AND YOUR HIJACKING OF THE FESTIVE SEASON BELONGS IN THE FUCKING SEA.

The Houses of Parliament

A giant clubhouse made out of gold and diamonds where a select group of self-serving wankers meet up and organize our lives for us, while forgetting how they got there in the first place. MPs, Lords – they're all as bad as each other, eating subsidized food and drinking cut-price booze while cutting our tax credits and flogging our nationalized utilities to anyone with a few bob to invest.

Not only do we pay their wages and exorbitant expenses, we're now also facing a mahoosive repair bill for their clubhouse, as it is on the brink of falling down around their puffed-up ears.

A recent report said that essential renovations could cost as much as £7 billion and take three decades to complete if Parliament's inhabitants don't get out of there for six years. Where will they go? How will they find troughs big enough for all their snouts? Will they have to leave London and live in the provinces? Oh, the humanity!

WHERE SHALL WE HOUSE THEM WHILE THE REPAIRS ARE BEING DONE? THAT'S RIGHT – IN THE FUCKING SEA.

Big Ben

Not only are the Houses of Parliament crumbling away like a digestive biscuit, it seems that Big Ben is fucked as well, with repairs needed that could cost a mighty £40 million.

I'm not a science expert but I'm pretty sure that you could remove its hands and just project the time on to its face using lasers from a building across the road. That'd set you back £500k at the most, assuming that the price of lasers is coming down. I know that memory sticks are getting cheaper, and a laser is fundamentally the same thing, right?

But wait! This is about more than just some mere cosmetic pissfartery – a report on the future of Big Ben suggested that we could end up being a global laughing stock if the clock falls silent.

About the repairs, it said: 'There are major concerns that if this is not carried out . . . the clock mechanism is at risk of failure with the huge risk of international reputational damage for Parliament.'

You can imagine the sniggers from the Belgians and the Nigerians at the next United Nations cocktail party – 'Those British idiots; not only is their parliament filled with greedy, heartless chancers, they can't get their fucking clock to work either!'

HOW ABOUT WE STRAP SOME EXPLOSIVES TO BIG BEN, KNOCK IT OVER ON TO THE HOUSES OF PARLIAMENT, FLATTEN THE FUCKING LOT AND DUMP THE RUBBLE IN THE FUCKING SEA BEFORE BUILDING A HOMELESS SHELTER INSTEAD?

Asking terminally ill people when they're expecting to die

When a friend or relative is visiting from afar, there's always that awkward moment when you ask them how long they're staying for. Sometimes it can offend, as they might think that you're trying to get rid of them (Christ, let's face it, you are).

Could be worse, though – at least you're not quizzing them over how much longer they'll be alive. You'd have to be an officer of the Department of Work and Pensions to be as cold and heartless as that.

You can add that one to the long list of breathtaking events that have happened under Iain Duncan Smith's reign of horror at the DWP – terminally ill welfare claimants were actually being asked when they were expecting to cark it. Face to face, by professional assessors.

Frank Field MP wrote to IDS about it all, describing it as 'intrusive and painful questioning'. Me, I'd have gone further and put it 'up there with the worst crimes of Pol Pot'.

BENEFITS ASSESSORS SHOULD BE ASKED HOW LONG THEY'D EXPECT TO SURVIVE ONCE THEY'VE BEEN CAST INTO THE EMPATHY-FREE KINGDOM THAT IS THE FUCKING SEA.

A typical day on Twitter

Twitter used to be really good. Its simplicity was its brilliance when it first became popular – scores of people would sign up, nervously dip their toe into its waters and gradually find like-minded folk, who they would then hang out with. Bonds were formed, lifelong friendships made, and some people even got married as a result. It seemed too good to be true, and of course it was.

Here's how a typical day pans out on Twitter now . . .

- Noteworthy thing happens.
- Every half-baked smartarse on Twitter makes flaccid attempt at a joke about noteworthy thing, with the best ones widely retweeted. Spats break out as the best ones are stolen by Twitter jackals and passed off as their own, and any fun that existed is quickly sucked out of proceedings.
- If noteworthy thing is controversial, two sides are formed – representatives of each side then engage in hurling insults at the other over their stance for a minimum of thirty-six hours. Often this leads to a further sub-outrage which can potentially drag on for a week. All fun that existed has now completely evaporated.
- If noteworthy thing has any connection whatsoever with women's issues, hordes of anonymous trolls use it as their excuse to bombard various women with vile abuse for forty-eight hours, forcing them to either close their accounts in order to escape from the horror or write a blog piece about said abuse. Blog piece is then widely shared on Twitter, leading to a fresh round of war between interested factions.

- Celebrities (who aren't glued to Twitter 24/7) catch up with proceedings, tweeting about those good, initial jokes from a couple of days ago that everyone is now sick of seeing. Everyone rolls their eyes.
- Six days pass and the fifth-best from those original jokes appears on *Have I Got News For You*.
- Blog pieces are written about how Twitter is dying/out of control and how something must be done.
- New noteworthy thing happens.

START BEING FRIENDLY AND FUNNY AND CLEVER AGAIN OR GET IN THE FUCKING SEA, YOU ANGRY BUNCH OF FUCKHOLES.

Minute's silence, unnecessary deployment of

The tragic death of a celebrity can unite an entire nation in a fog of collective grief, like when Princess Diana died in 1997 and 92 per cent of the population instantly went fucking apeshit – and to be fair, we've never really recovered.

It all triggered a new wave of over-emoting, and now we're up to our necks in unending minute's silences whenever there's any kind of notable loss of life.

Sporting events are bearing the full brunt of this

hypersensitivity/mourning mania, seeing as how they're the places where lots of people congregate and can be seen to be really showing their sadness. On the telly and everything.

Fast forward to 2024 and there'll be a minute's silence at the FA Cup Final because someone shat themselves on the Megabus on the way there.

IT'S FUCKING QUIET IN THE SEA – GET YOURSELVES IN AND HAVE A GO IF YOU DON'T BELIEVE ME.

People who marry their pets, objects or themselves

Getting married isn't all it's cracked up to be – it means you've almost always got someone lurking around you with their sudden movements and unexpected questions. Hardly ideal, but at least they'll keep you warm in bed at night.

But it's beyond baffling when people betroth themselves to something that isn't another like-minded human being. Batshit mental, to be more precise.

Take Amanda Rodgers, who married her dog Sheba in Croatia, in a service which was attended by 200 people. Now, I don't know if Amanda is batshit mental or not, but what I do know is that she was subsequently interviewed by Phillip Schofield on *This Morning* wearing a hat with a little veil on the front. Make your own judgement.

Or consider the plight of Yasmin Eleby of Houston,

Texas – she made a pact with herself when she was thirty-eight, deciding that if she wasn't hitched by the age of forty, she'd trot down the aisle with herself and put a ring on her own finger. Fucking hell – talk about not giving yourself much of a deadline. If you can't find someone, *anyone* who'll marry you by the time you're thirty-eight, you're probably not going to pull it off in the next twenty-four months.

In the end, Yasmin walked down the aisle arm in arm with her mother in what was referred to as a 'spiritual' service, as it isn't legal to marry yourself. Batshit mental? Who are we to judge?

Then there's Chris Sevier of Florida, who kicked right off when the authorities in Utah wouldn't let him be joined in holy matrimony with his porn-filled laptop, which he argued was better than any woman.

He said: 'I approached the Utah clerk to have a marriage licence issued for me and my machine-spouse. The clerk denied my request for a marriage licence . . . my object of affection was outside the scope of the narrow definition.

'If gays have the right to marry their object of sexual desire, even if they lack corresponding sexual parts, then I should have the right to marry my preferred sexual object.'

GET IN THE FUCKING SEA AND SEE IF YOU CAN FIND A MERMAID WHO'LL SHACK UP WITH YOU, YOU BUNCH OF FUCKING HEADCASES.

Poverty porn telly

Ah, reality television. Hovering a magnifying glass over the real world for all of us to enjoy in the comfort of our homes. Or, helping to amplify tensions in society through the inaccurate portrayal of noteworthy groups of people? It's one of those two, probably somewhere in the middle. Anyway, shush because *Benefits Street* is on, and last week's ended with Tony stuffing a trolley jack up his coat in Halfords.

Peering at folk who are struggling to exist while in a maelstrom of extreme poverty is the new *Generation Game* or *Bob's Full House* and is great for those water-cooler moments at work the next day – especially if you're looking to suss out just which of your colleagues are devoid of empathy and secretly read the *Daily Mail* on the bus in each morning.

We're probably just scratching the poverty porn surface at this point. As long as there's a demand for telly about poor people, there'll be desperate TV companies busting a gut to give the viewers what they want. Harder, poorer, worser.

Coming soon (probably to Channel 5) . . . *Benefits Autopsy*. Gaze in wonder at a dead poverty person having their corpse sliced open as a pathologist tries to work out what they died from.

'Hmmm . . . lots of tar in the lungs . . . but not from ordinary cigarettes. This tar is poverty tar probably from some unlicensed Eastern European cigarettes that have been smuggled into the UK by a criminal and sold at a lower than market price, thereby avoiding paying tax to the Queen and propping up society. This woman deserved to die. Next!'

There'll be a reality show where they recreate the Victorian workhouse before long, filled with actual benefits claimants. Just as a 'social experiment' you understand – nothing sinister. There certainly won't be any government officials keenly watching and making notes, oh no . . .

HOW ABOUT A REALITY SHOW WHERE CYNICAL TV EXECUTIVES ARE CONDEMNED TO LIVE IN THE FUCKING SEA? WE'D ALL WATCH THAT.

The British high street

Is it . . .

(a) a sacred part of the fabric of UK society where red-hot retail action traditionally happens?

(b) an accurate barometer of the nation's economic strength?

(c) a run-down row of identikit chain stores, pound shops, boarded-up units, charity shops that might not even be for actual charities, chuggers, beggars and thieving fuckers?

In a way, it's all three . . . but mostly the third one.

Wander down any British high street in the middle of a Saturday afternoon and marvel at the people there.

Thousands of them. They're the sort of people who think going to the shops in the middle of a Saturday afternoon is a fun way of doing things. They're the enemy within.

GREASED MEAT SCRAPINGS IN BUNS, SLAVE-MADE CLOTHES AND 'DO YOU NEED ANY HELP THERE?' IN EVERY SIN-GLE FUCKING SHOP YOU WALK INTO CAN ALL GET RIGHT IN THE FUCKING SEA.

Bollocks job titles

Everyone needs to feel special these days, and if that means pimping up your job title to make you sound more special than you really are, then fuck it, let's do it. It's why you'll see a sign on the door of your local Sub-way, advertising a role as 'sandwich artist' and why Hyundai call their sales people 'product angels'.

It's why German DJ Chris Montana describes him-self as an 'intercontinental party architect' and why make-up sales people are now being called 'beauty ambassadors'.

Fancy a career change, starting over as an 'education centre nourishment consultant'? You can call yourself that if you want to but your pals will still refer to you as a dinner lady.

GET IN THE FUCKING SALINE-BASED LIQUID EXPANSE, YOU PRICKS.

The fucking state of this – roping charities into a list of the worst things in the modern world. And yet there's no reason not to. They did this to themselves.

Over a hundred towns have now banned these bounding, over-friendly human parasites from their streets, such is the level of irritation that their presence causes.

They see you coming, they see you adjusting your route down the path unnaturally in order to avoid them, they see you staring at the ground in order to dodge making any kind of eye contact with them, and yet they *still* try to engage you in conversation as a preamble to getting your bank details and relieving you of £5.99 a month, some of which will go to badgers with brain AIDS.

You didn't even know badgers got brain AIDS until they stepped into your path! Why did they have to fuck up your day with their education and awareness-raising? Ignorance is bliss, right? Fuck off away from us!

THE MOST CHARITABLE THING TO DO WOULD BE TO GRAB YOU BY YOUR BRIGHTLY COLOURED CHARITY TAB-ARDS, WHISK YOU AROUND AND AROUND IN THE AIR AND THEN HURL YOU IN THE DIRECTION OF THE NEAR-EST FUCKING SEA.

The banks

Almost a decade after the global financial crisis that was *caused solely by the reckless greed of the banks*, we've got food bank use through the roof, child poverty off the chart, hard-working families losing out because George Osborne is shit at sums, and disabled people dying because some cold-hearted fuckmonster with a clipboard and a checklist has decided they're not actually disabled even though they had to get an unpaid carer to open the door and let them in so they could carry out the assessment in the first place.

Meanwhile, over in BankLand, shit is just carrying on as it did before, with perhaps a little bit more discretion being applied than ten years ago. There's certainly no bankers sleeping in cardboard boxes on the streets and none of them have been forced to pack up their stuff and move house because they can't make their meagre income stretch to cover the near-satanic bedroom tax bill.

To be fair, though, all the shitty stuff didn't happen in the high-street banks, where our wages are kept. No, the levels of skullduggery there are far lower – just the stuff we're used to, like eye-watering charges for going overdrawn, automated tills or the option to wait forty-five minutes to speak to a human (who'll be mainly focusing on selling you a financial product that you don't need once your actual query has been shoddily dealt with).

Enjoy their adverts, though – the ones with the terrible acting from the highly paid sports stars. Those bank charges I mentioned have helped to fund them, so drink up the ineptitude while you wonder why you can't afford to go out tonight.

Banks – like some kind of visual trick, they're complete and utter cunts no matter which angle you peruse them from.

PUT THEM IN THE FUCKING SEA. ALL OF THEM.

Streetwalking idiots

It's beyond belief that the number of people admitted to hospital after being punched in the back of the head for streetwalking idiocy isn't in the thousands.

There are crimes against society being committed every day on our pavements, with barely any justice being doled out. Walking three abreast, trudging along at less than two miles an hour, veering aimlessly while peering at a mobile phone; each and every one of them is surely a punchable offence, and yet we grind our teeth, mumble angrily under our breath and continue to allow it to happen.

YOU FUCKERS WILL SOON PICK UP THE PACE WHEN YOU'VE BEEN DISPATCHED INTO THE FUCKING SEA.

How did we reach a place where the festive season isn't officially under way until a department store has unveiled its traditional Christmas ad? An ad that is always anticipated as though it'll be the most important audio-visual piece of work since *Citizen Kane*, when it's really just a cloying lump of sentimental shite soundtracked by a twee voice lisping a song you really used to love but that is now fucked for ever.

Every single year without fail, acres of column inches are devoted to the John Lewis Christmas advert, what it means to us as humans and consumers and what it means for the advertising industry as a whole. Pah – 'industry'.

On Twitter, people use the advert as a gauge, to measure how much they can still feel, according to how much sadness and crying it made them do. It's become some kind of emotional MOT for people who spend the rest of the year casually dismissing photos of refugees that have been washed up on beaches, or gruesome news stories from America such as the one about the man who stored twenty-one vaginas in his freezer.

Get through a year of that shit and if you can still shed a tear at the John Lewis ad, you're okay to carry on as a human being. Further horrors will be along for you to glaze over at shortly.

It's not even as though the adverts are improving with age – the only one I can genuinely remember is the one where the little kid opens the present on Christmas Day and there's the severed head of his wife inside the box (although I might be blurring that memory with one of a film I once saw).

The most recent one was a bit of a departure, though – unless I misinterpreted it, it seemed to star the ghost of Jimmy Savile peering down at a young girl from heaven. Now just how the fuck is that supposed to be festive?

STOP IT. IT'S JUST A FUCKING ADVERT. SHUT THE FUCK UP ABOUT IT OR GET YOURSELF INTO THE NEAREST FUCK-ING SEA.

Suicide pedestrians

There's a new super-breed of human being out there that has no fear of being killed to death by a couple of tonnes of moving metal and glass. Quite happy to abdicate all responsibility for the continuance of their existence (or packing some kind of death wish), they think nothing of stepping out into the road without looking left *or* right first, assuming that drivers will recognize their right of way and brake suddenly, allowing them to get to where they need to be.

If they were ever taught the Green Cross Code as kids, they've either forgotten it or are refusing to acknowledge it, instead putting their faith in some kind of higher power to stop them from being mangled up by a bus and forced to breathe their last while lying on the tarmac and looking at their own spleen.

Why can't there be a law that says we can just mow these fuckers down? No? Just one day a year then? Go on – it'll thin out the idiot numbers a bit, and everyone wins.

TRY WANDERING AIMLESSLY INTO THE FUCKING SEA AND SEE HOW LONG YOU LAST, DICKHEADS.

Online petitions

'Please sign our online petition – it's about the government and all the bad things the government do and when we get 20,000 signatures on it we're going to present it to the government and we believe that they'll read it and understand why we're so cross and they'll stop doing all the bad things and we'll all suddenly start living in a fairer nicer society so please sign it please.'

Go fuck yourself – anyone who thinks that anything ever got achieved through an online petition needs to be waterboarded in a toilet filled with mind bleach.

The only purpose of an online petition is for certain people to be able to make it look as though they're doing something of worth, while getting their face in the spotlight. You've got more chance of changing the world by tying a note to the leg of a dead cat and dropping it down the chimney of 10 Downing Street.

The absolute worst are the ones that set up jokey online petitions aimed at achieving something unrealistic or trivial, such as the one launched when Phil Collins announced he'd be coming out of retirement and making a new album.

'Stop him,' cried some ridiculous internet knobheads, as they launched their petition with a light whimper. About 1,000 people signed it in the end, and Phil Collins is still at large. In fact, he could probably afford to have each and every one of the petition's signatories killed and he'd barely notice the dip in his bank balance. And no one would blame him if he did.

IF THERE'S AN ONLINE PETITION FOR ONLINE PETITIONS TO GET IN THE FUCKING SEA, SHOULD WE SIGN IT? THIS IS CONFUSING.

Motoring cunts

Excessively slow drivers that do 17 mph in a 30 mph zone, wankers who don't bother to use their indicators, pricks with personalized registration plates that have the slightest possible connection to their real name, fuckers who stick plastic eye lashes to their headlights, morons with 'powered by fairy dust' stickers clagged to their rear window, cunts who drive around with a mobile phone glued to their earhole, lorries that overtake other lorries on the motorway and take eight minutes to slowly crawl past them, people who park like utter cunts. Fuck the lot of you. Fuck you in the eye.

YOU'RE ALL SO FUCKING FECKLESS THAT YOU WON'T EVEN NOTICE AS YOU AMBLE YOUR CARS DOWN TO THE BEACH, ACROSS THE SAND AND DEEPER AND DEEPER INTO THE SEA. GOOD. FUCK OFF.

Earth's Fifty Worst Humans: Part 1

50 Dr David Starkey

Although he's a doctor, if David Starkey sat across a desk from you with a stethoscope around his neck and tried to diagnose what ailed you, chances are you'd either shit yourself with fear or chance your arm and try to stick his pen in the side of his neck.

It's okay though – he isn't a medical doctor, but one that knows about history and that.

Starkey doesn't inspire what you might call 'adulation' – he was born with two club feet, suffered from polio as a child and had a nervous breakdown in his early teens. I'm not a psychologist but perhaps that catalogue of childhood misfortune helped to make him into the empathy-free dickwad that he is today.

Although he is only seventy, the picture of him on Wikipedia looks as though it was taken in the 1930s rather than the 1980s, and he should probably sue them for emotional distress.

Starkey is regularly referred to as the rudest man in Britain, although if I could devote a couple of years towards training myself up, I'd love to go head to head with the fucker.

In recent years, he's positioned himself as something

of an expert on black youth culture and women histor-
ians, despite being an elderly white man, and his
appearances on *Question Time* do nothing for the collective blood pressure of the viewing audience.

HISTORY WILL NOT BE KIND TO YOU,
STARKEY – IT WILL REGARD YOU AS A
FUCKING CHUMP WHO ENDED UP FLOUN-
DERING IN THE FUCKING SEA.

49 *William Hague*

You can always judge a man by the way he conducts
himself in a pub and when you look at William Hague
you can easily imagine him putting his money down in a
puddle of ale on the bar rather than handing it directly
to the bartender.

He's got form when it comes to boozing, though, and
he once boasted of drinking up to fourteen pints of beer a
day as a teenager. That's typical Tory language at play – 'up
to' could mean as many as fourteen or as few as two.

He certainly doesn't look the sort who might be able
to neck fourteen pints, whether it be beer or even water.
He comes across more as the type who will have three
halves in his dinner hour then go back to work and
spend half the afternoon heaving his guts up into the
cleaner's bucket and worrying that his wife will smell his
breath when he gets home.

But is that enough to warrant a place in Earth's fifty

worst humans? Hmmm... he once wore a baseball cap with his surname across the front of it, so I'm saying yes.

OKAY, SO YOU'RE HARDLY HITLER, BUT THE SEA WILL WELCOME YOU WITH OPEN ARMS, YOU TWAT.

48 Kerry Katona

Who knew it would come to this when she appeared as a cute, gobby member of Atomic Kitten? Not me – it all seemed destined to play itself out in nine months culminating in a job at a bingo. But no.

Katona's life story has taken on a life of its own, and is now more epic than the Bible itself. Marriage, baby, split, breakdown, trampoline purchase, marriage, breakdown, split, baby, split, trampoline repossession, marriage, baby, baby, split, breakdown, marriage, marriage, hasty annulment, baby, breakdown, purchase of a depressed peacock called Trevor, split, marriage, baby, breakdown.

She's like the Stocks app on the iPhone – we all want rid of it but there doesn't seem to be a way of making it happen.

WHY WON'T YOU STOP? WHY DO YOU CONTINUE TO HAUNT US? ONLY A LONG SPELL IN THE FUCKING SEA WILL BRING AN END TO OUR DECADES OF UTTER TORTURE UNDER YOUR REIGN OF TERROR.

47 Josie Cunningham

'HI! My names Josie Cunningham. If you're reading this, then its quite likely you have read something about my life that has impacted youin either a positive way, but most likley negativley.' (*sic*)

That's the introduction to Josie's Moonfruit website, and it's about the most sedate and coherent message she's put out there in the eighteen months or so that she's tormented us via the twin attack mediums of the tabloid press and Channel 5 documentaries.

Initially famous for having a boob job on the NHS, she's gone on to become something of a one-woman shockwave, pumping out babies, causing outrage wherever possible and even appearing in court on a revenge porn charge.

Her crime? Posting a pic of her ex with a cartoon mushroom covering his balls. She'd removed his head so that he couldn't be identified, but even so, he claimed that it caused him anxiety attacks and all that other shit that people say these days.

Perhaps there should be some sympathy for Josie, though – after all, she knuckled down and got herself a job in a Walsall tanning salon not so long ago but was sacked on day one after it was pelted with eggs by protestors.

She's an enigma wrapped in a conundrum wrapped in a riddle topped off with £5k worth of NHS silicone implants . . . and she needs to be stopped.

EVEN AFTER YOU'VE BEEN TOSSED INTO THE BRINY, YOU'LL STILL PROBABLY FIND A WAY TO USE IT TO GET IN THE 'MEDIA SPOTLIGHT' – BUT FUCK KNOWS WE'LL HAVE FUN FINDING OUT. IN YOU FUCKING GO.

46 Olly Murs

Permanently sporting the grin of a child that's just been handed a free trifle, Murs knows that he's the luckiest little boy in the village. Unerringly mediocre at everything he does (singing, dancing, TV presenting and wearing a series of hats), his rise to the very, very top (well, presenting *The X Factor*) has been as chilling as it has been inexplicable.

But why the sea? Why not just leave him alone? After all, he isn't harming anyone.

There was one specific incident that makes him seaworthy – in April 2015, at Liverpool's Anfield ground, during the minute's silence for the victims of the Hillsborough disaster. For reasons known only to himself, Murs chose to spend that solemn minute with his match ticket held between his teeth.

On Twitter, his idiot customers rose up as one to defend him against his critics. He wasn't being disrespectful they howled – where else was he supposed to put his ticket? Erm, his hand? His pocket? The floor? Anywhere else except *in his fucking mouth*.

Perhaps his hands were full, they argued? With what – his cock? Was he wanking during a minute's silence? It was a spectacular night for fans of gawping at morons.

It also means that, from now on, if you're at a funeral and you see someone with the order of service between their teeth just as the coffin is being carried in, they're an Olly Murs customer. He made this acceptable.

So *that's* why he's going in the sea. Well, that and the fact that he exists and is being allowed to thrive, like a light-entertainment fungus.

CONGRATULATIONS, MURS, FOR PROV-ING BEYOND ALL DOUBT THAT 'ANYONE CAN MAKE IT' – EVEN A HAT-WEARING SHEET OF HUMAN PAPER LIKE YOUR-SELF. NOW GET IN THE FUCKING SEA, YOU RIDICULOUS CUNT.

45 Nick Clegg

This slippery fucker managed to sneak away like some kind of gas after the job had been done and dusted, didn't he? By 'job', I mean 'enabling Cameron and his fucko toff pals to get into power and set their Thatcher tribute group act loose on the poor, bewildered general public'.

Remember May 2010, when the wretched coalition was formed and its dual leaders held a little press confer-ence/soirée in the garden of 10 Downing Street? Clegg and Cameron were stood there, both sipping on glasses of orange juice and looking exactly like the couple of cunts they both obviously were.

Clegg could have done it all differently and shacked up with Labour for his coalition – it wouldn't have been perfect, but it probably wouldn't have resulted in chronically ill people killing themselves after being told they were fit for work when it was screamingly apparent that they weren't.

That's just part of your legacy, Clegg, but it's enough for the small amount of space that I've got here. Your actions directly led to the deaths of people who had nowhere else to turn. Big round of applause for you.

At the very least, I hope you struggle to sleep at night. Post-traumatic stress disorder is probably too good for you.

YOU ARE THE CUNT WHO OPENED PANDORA'S BOX THANKS TO YOUR LUST FOR POWER AND NOW YOUR ONLY OPTION IS TO FORM A COALITION WITH THE FISHES AT THE BOTTOM OF THE FUCKING SEA.

44 Duncan Bannatyne

It's the eyes. Look at his eyes. Dark, sly, scouting the room for an opportunity, usually an opportunity to invest in a company that makes edible doorknobs or environmentally friendly clown trousers, or a range of crayons made out of discarded hen's tits or kissy-lips for household radiators or some kind of spunk-deflection mask for kinky couples or a Womble incinerator or khaki flannelette bikinis or some Wotsits that an entrepreneur has filled up with hot butter.

He's got the look and dress sense of a failed gangster and is one of those blokes who makes jokes that only he thinks is funny.

Possibly worst of all is the fact that he has named his string of gymnasiums after himself, which is off-putting to say the least. What's the message here – do your running, star jumps and iron-pumping and you too could soon be slim, tanned, slightly oily and photographed in a tabloid newspaper at least once a year dressed in a white linen suit that makes everyone feel a bit weird?

GET IN THE FUCKING SEA YOU SLIPPERY GOBSHITE.

43 Gary Barlow

It's no coincidence that Gary Barlow only seems to thrive under a Tory government. Take That's heyday came when John Major ruled the land and even then, among the white heat of teeny megastardom, Barlow was nothing if not a pop version of the grey-faced PM.

Dull, functional, he was the sort of bloke you'd take home to meet your parents, only to regret it when he started banging on about the Maastricht Treaty, cone hotlines and the indisputable truth that no one ever got anywhere in life without working *really* hard.

Then New Labour came along and suddenly Barlow was on the bones of his arse, albeit inside a huge mansion. He gained even more weight, his hair fell out, and his eyeballs turned to stone (might be misremembering some of those finer details).

Hey presto – as Labour faded in popularity, back came Barlow, re-energized, brimming with vigour and armed with a satchel filled with a bunch of soporific tunes that his jaded former audience had grown into.

All of this has got me thinking that if Tony Blair was God, maybe Barlow was Satan. Ha ha ha ha ha ha! No – that analogy doesn't work.

Fast forward to the present day, and we're pretty much living in Barlow's Britain. Iffy tax-paying arrangements are met with a roll of the eyes and a 'What can you do, eh?' and 60 per cent of what was originally Take That is capering around in enormo-venues, churning out their new range of chugging hits and not doing all that much dancing.

Not only that, Barlow has developed a nice sideline in turning up at people's weddings and banging out a song, banking himself some points with God and making a whole host of bridegrooms feel a bit shit.

None of this would have happened if we'd just fucking left it alone in Iraq.

PAY YOUR FUCKING TAX AND THEN GET IN THE FUCKING SEA, WHERE MAYBE YOU CAN TURN UP AT THE WEDDING

OF A PAIR OF CRABS AND FUCKING
RUIN IT WITH YOUR MOCK-SENTIMENTAL
CROONING AND YOUR INFURIATING
MATEYNESS.

42 Professor Bowie

In 2015, the British education system is at a crossroads.
The policies of the Tory government mean that in a
decade or so there will be no new jobs of any worth to
be had.

Sure, it'll be easy enough to get yourself sixteen hours
a week in a call centre, fielding hundreds of complaints
from customers who have been sent the wrong trainers
because some other poor sod in a warehouse made a
mistake due to the fact that his zero hours contract stipu-
lates that he has to pick more trainers per shift than is
physically possible.

But we need to aspire to more than that. The education system needs to take the current generation and lift
them up, providing them with skills for the future.

Oh hello – here comes Will Brooker from London's
Kingston University. Perhaps he is the man we're looking for to lead us into the dark, scary tunnel of the mid
twenty-first century.

Ah, shit, no – Will's too busy spending an entire year
living as David Bowie instead. He's adopting his eating
habits, reading the same books he reads, and dressing in
his clothes. He'll even sample the star's dubious 1970s

diet of milk, red peppers and cocaine (only the cocaine is being substituted for energy drinks).

This is all fucking valuable research – in the future, when we want to know how David Bowie lived, Will's findings will be our first port of call. There'll be no need to refer to the acres of writing that other people have done about Bowie, and the various highly regarded biographies will be redundant.

Instead, we'll just have a look at Will's blog. It'll all be there.

YOU'VE BROUGHT THE ENTIRE CON-CEPT OF EDUCATION INTO DISREPUTE WITH YOUR LAZY, ATTENTION-SEEKING FUCKWITTERY – GET IN THE FUCKING SEA, 'PROFESSOR'.

41 Bear Grylls

It's easy to be suspicious of people like Grylls. So many questions arise – what is he, where did he come from, what does he want, why is he called 'Bear'?

In addition, his sister Laura is a 'cardio-tennis coach', which itself adds another question to our list.

But Grylls isn't seabound for being called Bear. Nor is he headed there for his long list of 'look at me' bullshit stunts – like the time he rowed naked along the Thames in a homemade bathtub, or the time he paramotored (you'll have to look it up) over Everest.

One of his biggest career breaks was when he fronted the Army's anti-drugs campaign. Now call me a wuss, but if I was serving in Her Majesty's Forces in an era when assorted prime ministers thought it was a good idea to send soldiers to a whole host of war zones and scenes of argy bargy around the globe, I'd be fucking desperate to suck hard on a bifter at the end of a day's battling.

Grylls isn't even featured here because of his obsession with the use of shit and piss as part of his 'survivaling' TV shows. Not only has he wrapped his urine-soaked T-shirt around his head to help stave off the desert heat, drunk urine that he'd saved up in a rattlesnake skin, supped the faecal liquid from elephant dung, scoffed deer droppings and used a bird guano/water enema for hydration, he also recently made actor Michelle Rodriguez eat a mouse that had been stewed in her own piss. Arguably his greatest crime of all.

Why the fuck is he obsessed with surviving in the wilderness? He's the son of a Tory MP and went to Eton. There's more chance of him being strangled to death by his own dick than there is of him genuinely finding himself struggling to survive in some jungle or other, unless he goes looking for it.

No, the sole reason that Grylls needs to be fired into the ocean (which the fucker would probably secretly enjoy) is because of his alarm clock policy. In an interview with NBC News, he said, 'I never call it an alarm clock, because I figure that's negative. I call it an opportunity clock!'

An. Opportunity. Clock. You utter fucking dick.

GET IN THE FUCKING SEA, GRYLLS, WHERE YOUR SURVIVAL CHANCES WILL BE HAMPERED DUE TO THE FACT THAT THE PISS THAT SEEMS TO HAVE BECOME YOUR WEIRD LUCKY MASCOT WILL BECOME DILUTED WITH SALT WATER, RENDERING IT UNDRINKABLE, YOU FUCKER.

Trends

The Cheese Postie

This packet of utter fuckery is described as 'the world's first subscription grilled cheese sandwich service', as though we'd all been wandering blindly for centuries, confused and afraid because no one was bringing cheese toasties to our doors and we were either having to cobble them together ourselves or schlep along to wherever the nearest student-heavy pub was.

It promises artisan bread (a tried and trusted rage-trigger round these parts), delicious condiments, 'world-class cheese' (world-class? From the milk of, say, Usain Bolt?), butter (well, DUHH!) and 'unusual ingredients'.

Yeah? How unusual do you want to be with your ingredients? Otter's whiskers? Shredded pages from the 1975 *Guinness Book of Records*? Sweat from the brow of the bloke who runs the waltzer at the fairground?

THE INVENTORS OF THIS ABSOLUTE TWATTERY NEED TO BE ARRESTED AND CHARGED FOR TREASON ON THE BASIS THAT THEY ARE FUCKING ABOUT WITH THE QUEEN'S SACRED ROYAL MAIL . . .

OR JUST FOR BEING A PAIR OF COCK ENDS. EITHER WORKS – AS LONG AS THEY ARE SENTENCED TO TEN YEARS' HARD LABOUR PICKING BARNACLES OFF OF SHIPWRECKS AT THE BOTTOM OF THE FUCKING SEA.

Autoplay videos on websites

These days, navigating a web page is a bit like bomb disposal – one wrong move and you're completely fucked. Click on the wrong pixel or trace your fingertip over a certain part of your phone's screen and you're instantly up to your eyes in an advert you didn't want to see, or worse still an ad with a fucking video running in it.

One minute, you're happily reading Arsenal transfer speculation on the bus, the next minute, you and your fellow passengers are all recoiling in horror at the clanging chimes of doom emanating from the trailer for the new Jason Statham action wankfest.

At least we've got a fighting chance of avoiding the videos, though, which is increasingly annoying the advertisers. Which is why autoplay videos are becoming the norm. Now you can't even avoid their corporate shit-flinging – the fucking ads start up as soon as you open the page.

It's happening on social media as well, with autoplay vids creeping on to Twitter and Facebook. The absolute nadir came in August 2015, after a reporter and cameraman were shot dead at point blank range by a former colleague, as they were broadcasting live on a Virginia news show.

Tweets of the footage, of people taking their final breaths, were tweeted and, with autoplay running, it was often too late to scroll away before you saw what had happened.

THAT'S WHERE WE'RE AT NOW? ENFORCED VIEWING OF SNUFF MOVIES IN OUR HOMES AND ON OUR PHONES? GET IN THE FUCKING SEA.

One-handed watch

Somewhere in a darkened basement office, let's say in Geneva, a man sits with his fingertips pressed hard against the sides of his head. An anguished man, his mind is swimming with the task that he has been set – to reinvent the wristwatch.

The pressure is immense. He knows that the boffins at Apple are planning a watch of their own, a device that could change how we look at our wrists for ever.

His deadline hurtles towards him, but he's got nothing. Panicking, he blurts out the words 'one-handed watch!' and, not sure if what he has come up with is genius or lunacy, goes with it anyway.

His Genevan paymasters rate him and say they believe it could catch on. In truth, they haven't got a fucking clue either, because everyone everywhere is bluffing it.

Called the Uno 24, the face displays a twenty-four-hour clock instead of a twelve-hour one and just one hand instead of two, and you can have it for about £400.

IT IS LITERALLY THE MOST UP-ITS-OWN-ARSE WATCH THAT ANYONE COULD POSSIBLY COME UP WITH. YOU'LL WANT TO CHUCK IT STRAIGHT IN THE FUCKING SEA ONCE YOU REALIZE THAT IT'S JUST A SMALLER WRIST-BOUND VERSION OF THE CLOCK ON YOUR BOILER.

Insurance companies giving away toys

Home contents insurance is important, or so they tell us. Look around your house right now at all the pointless tat you've acquired over the years and you might start to disagree with what 'they' say. Think about it some more and you'll find yourself wishing that some crack-addled thief would kick your back door in and make off with it all.

But hey – that'd be okay because you're insured to the hilt, right? You went on that quote comparison website a few months ago, just so that you could get yourself a free meerkat like that talking one on the advert.

You did *what*? You genuinely invested in a financial product based on the fact that there was a fucking *toy* to be had as part of the deal? Man alive, you *deserve* to be burgled! Trouble is, though – when your house does get ransacked, your stupid insurance meerkat and your hopeless insurance robot will be the only fucking things that the thieves leave behind.

AND THE SMALL PRINT ON THOSE POLICIES THAT YOU GREEDILY SIGNED UP FOR JUST SO YOU COULD GET A BATTERY-OPERATED LAUGHING MON-KEY WILL STATE THAT YOUR CLAIM ISN'T VALID. GET IN THE FUCKING SEA, YOU DIM-WITTED, SHIT-TOY-COLLECTING CUNTS.

Wellness

Here, do some juicing. Here, strap this fucking thing to your leg so it'll tell you how many steps you've walked. Why aren't you sieving the cholesterol out of that ketchup? Have you examined your stools today? Did you know you can buy bags of pre-owned cyclists' blood on eBay now?

Words there that so many of us hear every single day, all spoken by wellness freaks. Wellness – a new catch-all term for health, fitness and all other branches of the life-prolonging industry.

And, make no mistake, it *is* an industry. I'd estimate that there's enough money made by wellness organiza-tions to buy a Nutribullet big enough to stuff up the sun's arse.

The fundamental question that isn't being asked here is: 'What's so fucking wonderful about being well?' There's so much energy being devoted to fucking wellness that it's a surprise people aren't dropping down dead in the middle of the street from the strain of it all.

Also, there's a lot to be said for being ill. Who among us wouldn't fancy a couple of weeks laid up in hospital with something only fairly serious, as long as we could be assured that we wouldn't be struck down with MRSA or C. diff?

Nothing chronic and nothing that some powerful drugs and a few bed baths won't put right. Oooh, and the potential weight loss . . .

PUT YOUR FUCKING WELLNESS IN THE FUCKING SEA – ILLNESS IS THE FUTURE.

The Vetrosexual

Apparently this is a younger, better-dressed version of the metrosexual. In case you're not sure what the metrosexual is, it's a guy (not a bloke) who isn't afraid to show his toes off on a weekday, is comfortable wearing a lavender scent in mixed company and knows how much at least three different balms cost off the top of his head. He is a five out of ten when it comes to cunnilingus.

Nothing major to worry about there, but now we have the vetrosexual to contend with as well.

Extensive research carried out by me up the Asda has concluded that no one even knows who or what the vetrosexual even is or what they stand for. It appears to be a word that has either been made up by some lazy twat at a fashion magazine or has been chucked out into the world as part of some kind of twisted challenge or bet. We shall dwell on this no further.

IS THE VETROSEXUAL A STRONG SWIM-MER? I FUCKING DOUBT IT SOMEHOW. SEA.

Slogan stencils in houses

Words are magical. Words bring our imaginations to life and can paint a million pictures. Not sure if that's why dickheads have started putting stencilled words all over their houses, though. It looks like they're living inside a graphic novel or a fucking crossword.

You must have seen them – they're the ones on the walls of all the slightly overpriced houses on Rightmove. Trite, shite slogans and phrases that mean fuck all and are really hard to scrape off once you become sick of the sight of them after a month.

I'm thinking about phrases like: 'Life isn't about wait-ing for the storm to pass . . . it's about dancing in the rain.' Or: 'Dance like no one's watching. Love like you've never been hurt. Sing like no one's listening. Live like heaven is on earth.'

They should be more realistic and try to represent everyday family living. Something like: 'If he puts the cereal bowls in the top half of the dishwasher again, where the mugs are supposed to go, I'll put the potato peeler in the side of his neck.'

Or: 'The youngest will be off to university in a couple of years and then it's just me and him left. Him with that throaty noise he makes when he laughs, his habit of switching the lights on and off before we go out and that haircut that makes him look like Bob Monkhouse. Kill me now.'

AN OCEAN-THEMED HOUSE WITH 'GET IN THE FUCKING SEA' SCRAWLED ON THE WALL IS ALL YOU NEED, TO REFLECT YOUR CONSTANT DISAPPOINTMENT AND IRRITATION AT YOUR SHIT LIFE.

Rainbow armpit hair

'Rainbow armpit hair is a thing,' tweeted *Stylist* magazine not so long ago, accompanied by a pic of a woman proudly showing off a bright green tuft that had sprouted from beneath her arm.

For all I know, *millions* of women are doing this rainbow armpit hair thing but are keeping it hidden under dark clothing, only unfurling their luminous secret once they're back home and have closed the curtains for the night.

That, or *Stylist* magazine are grasping at straws for something that might get them a bit of attention.

GET IN THE FUCKING SEA AND CHECK OUT THE STATE OF THE MERMAIDS' ARMPITS.

Content and fucking clickbait

Everywhere you fucking look – content. Formerly known as articles, features or even pieces, it's the stuff that makes up the newspapers, magazines and websites that we lazily gawp at.

There used to be a finite amount of content, which was good. You paid good money for a magazine or newspaper, it had a fixed number of pages, and you knew when it was finished because you'd run out of paper and words and that to look at.

Then along came the internet, with its fucking 'websites', and everything we'd become accustomed to got flipped on its head.

For one thing, we stopped paying – *brilliant*! Everyone loves free stuff, right? Not brilliant. So much of the free content we get on these fucking 'websites' is lazy, sloppy, uninspired cack. *No, not just like this book, you fucking shitehawk.*

Now, because we're not paying, web publishers need to make their cash from getting us to click on adverts, and the more content they can churn out the more clicks they can potentially get and the closer they can stay to keeping their heads above water.

So we're bombarded with shoddy, mindless bollocks in place of actual news, such as 'Here's 12 times Vladimir Putin looked like he was farting during Ukraine press conference' or attention-seeking, nuance-free opinion shit such as 'Why I think it's a good thing for horse meat to be force-fed to gypsy dole scroungers', designed to cause outrage and generate a million clicks before lunchtime.

Actually, I'd better just check that last one hasn't already been done by Katie Hopkins . . .

HERE'S A FUCKING CLICKBAIT HEAD-LINE FOR YOU – '27 DIFFERENT WAYS YOU CAN BE ROCKETED INTO THE FUCKING SEA'.

TL; DR

It stands for 'too long; didn't read' and is used on Twitter when discussing a lengthy piece of writing elsewhere. It's pretty much shorthand for saying 'I am a vacuous bell end with the attention span of a flea'.

In truth, it should be TAF; CBA as in 'thick as fuck: couldn't be arsed'.

STOP BEING PROUD OF YOUR IGNOR-ANCE AND GET IN THE FUCKING SEA.

Bitcoin

Possibly the future of global currency itself, possibly a passing fad dreamed up by a bunch of lads who've seen *Tron* too many times and hear their mothers' voices in their heads when they're wanking and they can't decide if they like it or not.

All of which begs the question: 'What the fucking fuck is a bitcoin?'

I'll try to be as clear and as brief as possible here – it's shit. Shit for cunts.

Okay, I'll elaborate if I really need to. Apparently, bitcoins are created as a reward for payment processing work in which users offer their computing power to verify and record payments into the public ledger. This is better known as 'mining', and 'miners' are rewarded with transaction fees and newly created bitcoins. So, it's like regular money, only way more ridiculous.

An increasing number of merchants are accepting bitcoins as the system becomes increasingly popular. That's the problem we've got here – a monetary system devised by and for bell ends is being legitimized by other bell ends who don't have the spine to tell these mining spods to go fuck themselves.

Entrepreneur Martijn Wismeijer is so enamoured of it all that he underwent the painful procedure of having near field communication chips embedded in his hands so that his bitcoin could be on his person at all times. If you ask me, he should have them jammed up his arsehole.

Bitcoin? Shitcoin more like.

THE SEA DOES NOT ACCEPT FUCKING BITCOIN. IN YOU FUCKING GO THEN.

Vacuum love couples

The expression of sweet, sweet love takes on many forms. Some people demonstrate their mutual devotion by getting matching tattoos, while others wear lockets containing a piece of hair clipped from the heads of their significant others. Takes all sorts, I suppose.

Then there's the ones that get photographed while they're coiled around each other and vacuum-sealed together in an airtight plastic bag. Yes, that's a thing.

It's all the brainchild of Japanese artist Haruhiko Kawaguchi, who took nearly eighty couples and trapped them in vacuum-sealed bags. The deranged bastards had to pose and hold their breath for ten to twenty seconds while Kawaguchi snapped a few pics of them.

It's a rum business. Don't try it at home. Or anywhere, for that matter.

YOU JUST LOOK LIKE A SUPERMARKET-BOUGHT HALF DUCK, READY FOR THE OVEN. GET IN THE FUCKING SEA INSTEAD.

Shower beer

Have you ever drunk beer in the shower? Don't even bother to answer that – (a) this is a book and a book can't hear you or read your lips; (b) of course you fucking haven't because drinking beer while you shower is not, and will never be, a thing that humans will do.

Right-thinking humans, that is – as we're learning, we're never that far away from some attention-seeking dickwad who will try and pass off any kind of left-field behaviour as being some sort of fad. Then they'll do a website and probably try and flog you stuff. Not like Get In The Sea. Get In The Sea is more of a necessary social movement.

According to the pricks on the internet (more specifically the American ones), drinking beer in the shower is now a trend. As trends go, it's about as random and as valid as, say, putting your TV in the middle of the garden, or eating a sandwich with your feet.

It's bollocks and it needs to be stamped out with extreme prejudice right now.

Having said that, I once drank two cans of Stella Artois in the space of thirty minutes in a piping hot bath while watching an episode of *Curb Your Enthusiasm* on a laptop, and it was one of the absolute high points of my entire life to date. Try it if you don't believe me.

TRY KNOCKING BACK A CAN OF BEER IN THE SEA, YOU TRY-HARD WANKERS.

School proms and limousines and all that shite

What are we doing to our children? The emergence of the school leavers' prom has got to be one of the worst developments for kids since they were made to work in coal mines when they were eight.

Leaving aside the fact that it all costs the already fiscally fucked parents squillions of quids for their younglings' outfits, hair appointments, limo hire and possible post-prom rehab, it all gives the teens a completely wrong idea about how life is going to be after they've walked out of the school gates for the final time.

Worse still, even the four-year-olds are having end-of-nursery proms now. Rather than a glitzy red-carpet party, they should be made to sit in the middle of an abandoned quarry and be shown films of broken grown-ups talking frankly and openly about the debt, disease and disaster that has destroyed their adult lives.

THERE'S NO REASON FOR THE FOUR-YEAR-OLDS TO BE DUMPED INTO THE FUCKING SEA – THEY CAN BE TAKEN INTO CARE AND ADOPTED BY PEOPLE WHO AREN'T FIXATED ON WASTING A SHITLOAD OF CASH ON FLASH CARS AND FILLING THE HEADS OF INFANTS WITH UNREALISTIC FANTASYLAND BULLSHIT. EVERYONE ELSE INVOLVED – IN THE FUCKING SEA.

New double-barrelled surnames

It's become quite the fashion in these here modern times for marrying couples to clang their surnames together post-wedding, creating a new, super-strength double-barrelled surname. If you're one of these people, please don't be too offended but you just might be some of the most self-absorbed motherfuckers currently at large on Planet Earth.

It might seem like a super, modern idea to crowbar your family names together, but what if you start a family? What happens if your kids grow up and fall in love with someone else who has been saddled with a two-part moniker by their idiot parents?

They're not going to have the luxury of double-barrelling *their* surnames as well, unless they want to raise the stakes even higher and go for a mouth-mangling quadruple-barrelled name.

'Congratulations to the newly-weds . . . Mr and Mrs Taylor-Watkins-Johnson-Harrison!' Fuck right off.

GET IN THE FUCKING SEA, YOU SELFISH, NAME-SQUIRRELLING BASTARDS.

Soft play for adults

The lines between childhood and adulthood are more blurred than they've ever been now, with self-awareness and shame seemingly things of the past. How else would you explain kids' soft play areas that are devoted solely to adults?

The Play Factory in Thornaby, Teesside, recently bowed to overwhelming public demand and hosted a session exclusively for the grown-ups, taking inspiration from shows like *I'm a Celebrity . . . Get Me Out of Here!* and *The Crystal Maze* and coming up with special challenges for the infantalized adults.

Adventure tasks, time trials, laser tag and races were all on the menu, instead of say, a cloud of highly poisonous gas. Manager of the venue Jenny Archer said she hadn't ruled out introducing alcohol to future sessions if the fun-loving fuckwads could prove that they could behave responsibly.

Alcohol? Fuck that. They've waived their rights to be treated as adults the minute they set foot in the ball pool. They can have rosehip syrup out of sippy cups and be spoon-fed a jar of Cow & Gate sweet potato and beef like all the other babies.

GET IN THE SEA YOU FUCKING PERVERTS.

The huggable toaster

Dreamed up and made real by London-based product designer Ted Wiles, this deranged contraption won't heat your slices of bread unless you hold it close and give it a bit of a cuddle first.

Fuck's sake – can I not just have some toast first thing in the morning without having to get embroiled in some kind of emotional trade-off with a kitchen implement? Does the butter need to be lightly kissed before I can spread it on top? Do I have to finger the raspberry jam to orgasm before I'm allowed some of that too?

JUST DO MY FUCKING TOAST OR GET IN THE FUCKING SEA, YOU NEEDY CUNT.

Adult colouring-in books

One of the more recent additions to the growing trend of twee mimsiness infesting the world of the grown-up, or more specifically, the grown-up who can't handle being one.

Cast your mind back to your grandparents. They probably had it fairly tough – Grandad worked in heavy industry and was always tired and sore from his labours, but he still had the time and patience to play football with you or read to you.

Meanwhile, Grandma could turn out an apple crumble that you can smell right now when you think about it and was a dab hand at darning your socks when they had a hole in them.

Their lives were hard – there was no central heating, so there were a couple of coal fires to tend to each and every day, but they got by. One thing's for sure, though – they would have rather died in a shameful suicide pact than waste their spare time fucking about with adult colouring-in books.

The very idea of actually published titles like *The Fairyland Adult Colouring Book* or *Love and Kisses – Beautiful Patterns to Colour* would have confused and disgusted Grandad into an aneurism.

LOOK – YOU'RE ADULTS, SO FUCKING ACT LIKE IT. YOUR LIFE NOW IS ALL ABOUT CANCER SCARES, BOUNCED LOAN REPAYMENTS, BLOCKED GUTTERING, PUTTING YOUR PARENTS IN CARE HOMES AND THE CREEPING REALIZATION THAT TIME IS SPEEDING UP AND THERE'S FUCK ALL YOU CAN DO ABOUT IT. STOP PRETENDING THAT YOU'RE SEVEN AGAIN. YOU DIDN'T EVEN ENJOY COLOURING-IN WHEN YOU WERE SEVEN, FOR FUCK'S SAKE. GIVE UP HIDING FROM THE SHITTY REALITIES OF YOUR LIFE. EITHER TACKLE THEM HEAD ON OR HURL YOURSELF INTO THE FUCKING SEA.

Bronde

Glamour magazine called it, 'the hair colour trend that's taking 2015 by storm' and they must be right because I can't think of any other hair colour trends of 2015 whatsoever. Bronde has fucking owned it – all the other hair colour trends are lying in the corner, shaking like shitting dogs.

Don't know what bronde is? You must be either bald, blind or an idiot. Or all three. Or two out of the three.

It's a lethal combination of both blonde and brunette, a hair colour equivalent of Tony Blair's 'Third Way' of politics, which has since been discredited and obliterated by Jeremy Corbyn's grey alternative. Okay, bad comparison.

Getting back to bronde, *Glamour* sought out the expert advice of Siobhan Jones, Colour Ambassador at Headmasters. No, I've got no idea, but if they're dealing with a Colour Ambassador, it's clear that *Glamour* aren't fucking about here.

Siobhan cites Kim Murray as the top bronde on the bronde scene (if indeed there is a bronde scene), saying: 'It's a really flattering bespoke colour and by combining her natural darker blonde with lighter ribbons around her hairline and ends, her eyes really stand out; it's a hue that really suits her!'

Can't afford that bronde look yourself? Go for a 'home bronde' – a bleached blonde barnet followed up with selective use of gravy browning. Own that bronde look, baby – it's your time to shine! Just don't go out in the rain.

EVERYONE KNOWS YOU CAN'T INVENT NEW COLOURS WITHOUT THE FULL APPROVAL OF THE UNITED NATIONS.

STOP BEING A CUNT IN ORDER TO FLOG
YOUR TWATTY HAIR DYE AND GET IN
THE FUCKING SEA.

Standing desks

Working in an office is a terrible state of affairs, on
an emotional level if nothing else. Constant exposure
to fuckwits who you despise is a surefire way of sending you hurtling towards either nervous collapse
or a substance abuse problem. And yet we give
these people the pleasant-sounding name of 'colleagues'.
Bleh.

Then there's the physical pressures as well. Sitting at
a desk all day long fucks you right up, apparently – this
is why office workers get measured up for special chairs
and bosses aren't allowed to throw stuff at them any
more.

But how can the office experience be improved?
Especially in a way that might seem a bit kooky, so that
bloggers would write about it? Say hello (or if you like,
fuck off) to the standing desk.

Becoming increasingly popular among bell ends, the
beauty of the standing desk is that it allows you the flexi-
bility and space to be able to move around. It's also
easier if you suffer from an itchy arsehole, but please be
discreet.

The only people in the world who should be allowed
to operate a keyboard while standing up are Jerry Lee

Lewis or Kraftwerk. Everyone else can sit the fuck back down again and stop trying to draw attention to themselves.

GET BACK ON YOUR FUCKING ARSE OR GET IN THE FUCKING SEA, YOU SHOWY WANKERS.

The mooted Apple car

One day we'll look back and laugh at things like the Ford Ka and the Renault Megane. 'Do you remember when loads of companies made cars?' we'll howl, while trading stories about steering wheels and having to be sober and alert enough to use the brakes and that.

By then (probably 2021), we'll all be in thrall to the car that Apple will have pioneered for us. Self-driving, it'll connect to all your other Apple devices by Bluetooth, and by then there'll be new devices that will probably be able to serve up portions of special Apple Porridge that are packed full of nutrients and that we'll inject straight into our eyeballs.

Body scanners will read our emotions and provide us with music or movies that they think we want to hear or see, and long journeys will be eased with massaging seats and a self-flushing Apple Potty that will eradicate the need for all the motorway service stations that Google bought up in 2019.

WHY WON'T YOU PSYCHO GADGET CUNTS STOP? WHAT DO YOU WANT – IS IT OUR BRAINS? IT IS, ISN'T IT – IT'S OUR BRAINS. YOU WANT TO REPLACE THE BRAIN OF EVERY HUMAN BEING ON EARTH WITH AN APPLE HARD DRIVE THAT CONTROLS OUR MOVEMENTS, REPORTS BACK WITH OUR BEHAVIOUR AND NEEDS CHARGING EVERY THREE HOURS. GET IN THE FUCKING SEA.

Letters by 'kids' that go viral

Being able to create 'viral content' is now almost as valuable as gold, platinum, myrrh or whatever it is that's inside golf balls. If you're a 'brand', and can come up with something that is shareable on Twitter and Facebook, you win all the prizes – the prizes being eighteen hours in the public eye and a minimal increase in your takings.

Anything will do as long as it'll get people looking in your direction, and using kids to tug on the heartstrings of the mealy-minded is a surefire way of winning the attention of the slack-jawed gonks of the internet.

One of the first examples of this shithousery was the letter from a 'three-year-old child' to Sainsbury's, asking why the tiger bread isn't called giraffe bread because it looks more like a giraffe than a tiger. The 'letter' spread like wildfire, and hey ho, the renamed bread was soon flying off the shelves – presumably some customers were frightened of it because they thought it was an actual fucking tiger.

Since then, the practice has spread to letters from eight-year-olds whining about sexist toys, to pictures on social media of homework that kids have supposedly done, with witty answers that seem to be more akin to those that a bored, lonely thirty-three-year-old parent might come up with.

I'm not accusing anyone of anything underhand here . . . but this shit needs to stop now.

'WHAT DID YOU DO AT WORK TODAY, DADDY?'

'I PRETENDED I WAS YOUR AGE AND WROTE A LETTER SO THAT LOTS OF PEOPLE WOULD LOOK AT IT ON THE INTERNET AND THEN WE'D SELL MORE BAKED SNACK TREATS.'

'YOU'RE A PRICK, DADDY. YOU BELONG IN THE FUCKING SEA.'

Air sex

You're familiar with the air guitar, yes? A brilliantly simplistic way of (a) allowing wannabe guitar heroes to live out their axe-wrangling fantasies without having to do any of the complicated stuff such as buy or learn to play a guitar, and (b) identifying complete wankers.

If only humanity had stopped at the air guitar instead of exploring other similar options. But no – now we have 'air sex' as well. Tragically, it's exactly what you'd expect – attention-starved shitehawks getting up on stage and performing sex acts on and with an invisible 'partner'. They even keep their clothes on, which is possibly a disappointment, although possibly not.

These writhing, moaning dickheads are almost certainly all virgins and that's the way it needs to stay, even if it means sectioning them and performing chemical castration on them.

YOU FUCKERS DESERVE TO BE BUMMED INTO OBLIVION BY A GHOST IN THE MIDDLE OF THE NIGHT AND THEN HURLED INTO THE FUCKING SEA.

The silent disco

If a disco happens but no one can hear it, does it even actually happen? Unfortunately, in the case of the silent disco, it very much does. For the uninitiated, it's a room full of people, all wearing wireless headphones with the music transmitted to them, thereby eliminating noise in the venue. This means you can have a disco in a place where noise is usually frowned upon, like the car park of a monastery or an intensive care unit.

But if you're riddled with paranoia or have gnawing trust issues, the silent disco is more like psychological torture. How do you know everyone else is listening to the same music as you? How do you know they're even listening to music at all? Perhaps they're all decoy-dancing while listening to a lecture that is all about you, listing all your failings as a human being and the most embarrassing moments of your futile life so far.

Enjoy the next 'silent disco' that you go to, eh?

SEE HOW YOU LIKE DANCING WITH YOUR HEADPHONES ON WHEN YOU'RE BOBBING ABOUT IN THE FUCKING SEA, YOU SMUG TWATS.

The hashtag costume

It's exactly what you'd expect – a lurid body stocking with a massive hashtag that sits across the front of your torso. To be seen wearing one in public is akin to handing out leaflets saying: 'I am beyond salvation, unable to realize that by choosing to wear this costume, I am marking myself out as one of society's most tragic members. My naivety knows no bounds. Keep a close eye on me, as I am almost certainly a threat to the equilibrium of you and yours around you. I don't even deserve the sweet release of death, even a really, really painful one.'

£15.99 on Amazon if you fancy your chances, you daft bastard.

DOES IT FLOAT? NO? GOOD! CHUCK IT IN THE FUCKING SEA.

GQ's *Politician of the Year award*

If you're in need of a pinpoint-accurate reading of all of the very worst social and cultural shit that this nation has to offer, you'll need to carefully study the *GQ* Awards. On one hand, they could be seen as a glittering showpiece occasion, aimed at bringing together the thrusting achievers of the past twelve months and highlighting them for their immaculately groomed, scent-wearing £800-watch-adorning readers.

On the other hand, they could be seen as a grotesque act of annual trolling, aimed at winding up the self-righteous gonks on social media and perpetuating the belief that there's no such thing as bad publicity.

Dig, if you will, the winners of *GQ* 's Politician of the Year award since 2008. In chronological order, we've got Boris Johnson, George Osborne, David Cameron, George Osborne again, Boris Johnson again, Boris Johnson *again*, Alex fucking Salmond and George Osborne *yet a-fucking-gain*.

Just why *GQ* have used the word 'politician' when 'cuntweasel' would be far more accurate is baffling, to be honest. For fuck's sake, they even made laser-eyed warmongerer Tony Blair the Philanthropist of the Year back in 2014.

GQ – SKILFULLY TURNING THE SPOT-LIGHT ON THE MEN WHO WANT TO SUCK ALL THE FUN OUT OF YOUR LIFE AND MAKING OUT LIKE IT'S A GOOD THING. GET THEM IN THE FUCKING SEA.

Water menus

Belfast's Merchant Hotel hit the headlines in 2015 when it unveiled a water menu. A fucking water menu. A fucking list of all the different kinds of water you can 'enjoy' while you're eating in their joyless fucking restaurant.

Sort of like a wine list, but completely devoid of every-thing that makes a wine list a valid concept. Water. Fucking water. The place even has a water butler, and what's more, he was seemingly happy to be named (outed even) as part of the publicity drive.

Justin Moore they call him. Justin Moore, the fucking water butler. Scuttling up to you in the dining hall of the Belfast Merchant Hotel and unveiling his fucking water menu for you, as you try to stifle your disgust. You'd rather be in the papers for being caught sodomizing a tractor, wouldn't you?

THE ONLY WATER MOORE AND HIS EMPLOYERS NEED TO BE FAMILIAR WITH IS IN THE FUCKING SEA.

The No Phone

You know what'd be, like, great? A mobile phone that didn't have *any* functions whatsoever. No calls, no texts, no internet, no camera, nothing. Just a thin, hopeless brick. Yeah, that'd be, like, a *statement* about mobile phones and the role they play in modern life. Just imagine it – it'd be shaped like a mobile, but it does absolutely fuck all. Wow. Genius.

It's real though. It's really happened. Some dickwad has gone to the trouble of manufacturing these rectangular lumps of nothingness and is actually selling them for cash money. Form a queue, idiots – here's someone who is waiting to take your coins right out of your hands with a great big smile slapped across his face while he's about it.

Your part of the deal? You'll have a useless slab of nowt clasped in your paw. But how will your friends keep in touch with you? Once they've seen you brandishing this piece of twat's equipment in public, that really won't be a problem for you any more . . .

DOES IT FLOAT? DOES THE FUCKER FLOAT? BECAUSE ALL IT'S GOOD FOR WOULD BE A RAFT FOR ANTS. GET IT IN THE FUCKING SEA AND FIND OUT.

Clothes with bits missing

Want a pair of jeans with massive sections cut out of the part that's supposed to cover your thighs? That'll be the thick end of £100. How about a mesh top that looks as though it's been pulled apart by rabid dogs? £150 to you.

STUPID ENOUGH TO FORK OUT FOR CLOTHING THAT ISN'T EVEN 100 PER CENT THERE? GET IN THE FUCKING SEA.

Bluetooth phone gloves

Always wanted to turn your gloved hand into a phone receiver, listening to a call with your thumb while speaking into your little finger? Now you can, as the Bluetooth phone glove has hit the market, to the delight of no one anywhere whatsoever.

Other than giving you the ability to make and receive calls into your hand like a fucking seven-year-old, there doesn't appear to be any noticeable benefit for owning this ludicrously ill-advised piece of tat. The only thing that's certain is that wearing them will make you more of a target for snowball-wielding schoolkids.

WHICH IS THE LEAST YOU DESERVE – THAT, AND A DIP IN THE FROZEN DEPTHS OF THE FUCKING SEA.

Wine for cats

Attention, lonely cat owners. Your cat is superior to you. It comes and goes and only chooses to live with you for as long as it is content with your company. If it gets a better offer, whoosh – it'll be gone.

This is your reality – you deny it by numbing your solitude with nightly overdoses of wine. Helpfully, some chancer has spotted a gap in the market and has produced wine for cats; a subtle blend of Cabernet grapes, vitamin C and catnip.

That's right – drink up your wine with your cat. Pretend it is your significant other. Talk to it about your day. It doesn't care. In fact, keep forcing the 'cat wine' on it and it'll be gone sooner rather than later.

Forget your cat. Let it go. Your heart is already broken. Focus on mending yourself. Stop it with the fucking wine all the time. This is your last chance.

OR JUST GET IN THE FUCKING SEA. THE ICY WATER WILL HELP YOU FORGET

YOUR PAIN, AND YOUR CAT WILL MOVE IN WITH THE OLD LADY AT NUMBER 65 BECAUSE SHE GIVES HIM FRESH FISH INSTEAD OF FUCKING CAT WINE.

Ye olde crafty television

The Great British Bake Off has got a lot to answer for – and I don't just mean the insidious creep of Paul Hollywood into the public's consciousness. Its raging success convinced telly bosses that there's a major appetite for shows about old-style ways of doing things, with the tweeness ramped up to the maximum.

The Great British Sewing Bee? Competitive sock-darning? Off you fuck, thank you very much. *The Great Pottery Throw Down*? You can get vases in Poundland now, so you can fuck off quickly as well.

They're not going to quit with this shite for a while yet, so brace yourselves for *The Great British Basket Weaving Fiasco* and *The Great British Leech Treatment Death Escapade* over the next few months.

WE CAN'T BE ARSED WITH MAKING STUFF FROM SCRATCH WHEN WE CAN JUST GET IT IMPORTED FROM CHINA FOR ABOUT 45P. GET IN THE FUCKING SEA WITH IT ALL.

Earth's Fifty Worst Humans: Part 2

40 *Danny Alexander*

The former Chief Secretary to the Treasury might well have been handed a knighthood only three months after being handed his arse by the voters in his former Inverness, Nairn, Badenoch and Strathspey constituency, but he can fuck off if he thinks his fancy new title is going to be acknowledged here.

It's hard to see what kind of public role Alexander can play following his electoral decimation – after all for five years we all saw him as the clueless, bumbling sap who was sent out by George Osborne on to the media landscape to soak up and try to bat away all of the tricky questions that the Chancellor's 'tough decisions' gave rise to. Tough decisions like . . . well, like fucking the poor on a grand scale.

For half a decade, Alexander was Gorgeous George's fall guy, stammering and blethering about policies that he probably didn't even agree with in the first place. It was as perfect an example of public school fagging (the traditional practice where younger pupils were required to act as personal servants to the most senior boys) as you're ever likely to see.

And yet, Alexander, a company man to the bitter end,

played his part, and now he's been rewarded with his knighthood.

IF THERE'S ANY JUSTICE, THE QUEEN WILL DO THE RIGHT THING AT HIS KNIGHTING CEREMONY AND SLICE ALEXANDER'S HEAD CLEAN OFF HIS SHOULDERS BEFORE JUMPING IN HER BENTLEY, RACING TO THE NEAREST CLIFF EDGE AND TOE-PUNTING THIS PITIFUL FUCKER'S SEVERED BONCE STRAIGHT INTO THE FUCKING SEA.

39 Jamie Oliver

It's hard to decide which of this fucker's many and varied public transgressions have earned him his place on this ultimate rundown of total shitheels – his fat-tongued verbalizations aren't strictly his fault (although he's rich enough to be able to afford some kind of tongue reduction) so that should probably be scratched from the list, but his chirpy mockney mannerisms make him a cast-iron sea contender.

Remember back in the early days, when the public fell headlong for him as he whizzed around on a scooter, giving it all the 'oi oi' and the 'happy days' to all and sundry as Toploader played on a loop in the background? A long time ago and possibly not enough on its own to warrant a one-way trip into the icy cold water.

Let us consider Oliver's more recent one-man nanny state campaigning, usually against stuff that is bad for us but that we quite enjoy, which only irritates us when he's trying to educate us.

His latest campaign is against the evils of sweet, tasty, addictive, beautiful sugar, the twat. Mind you, as the campaign was launched, he was still selling full-fat Coke in his gruesome restaurants. So some sugar is better than other sugar then?

Let's overlook the fact that he named his kids Daisy Boo Pamela, Buddy Bear Maurice, Petal Blossom Rainbow and Poppy Honey Rosie – but only because that crime against humanity is featured elsewhere in this book.

WE'RE ALL SICK OF THE SIGHT OF YOU, OLIVER – GET IN THE FUCKING SEA AND TRY LECTURING SOME KILLER SHARKS ABOUT THEIR DIETARY DEFICIENCIES. GO ON, GET UP REALLY CLOSE SO THEY CAN HEAR WHAT YOU'RE SAYING TO THEM.

38 Max Knoblauch

One of the problems with the fast-moving world of digital media is that it's filled with slow-moving fuckwits churning out stone-cold, space-filling shite. How else could you explain New York writer Knoblauch's woeful 'social experiment', where he went around dressed up as Prince George for a week?

That's right – he got himself some adult baby clothes made and spent five days twatting around in them, looking nothing like the heir to the throne but more like someone who should be on some kind of register.

You're probably dying to find out what he learned from all of it, right? Fuck all – that's what. 'New Yorkers do not care what you wear,' he concludes. Maybe they're just too polite to call you a cunt to your face.

Knoblauch? Knobhead more like.

WERE YOU STARVED OF ATTENTION AS A CHILD, YOU PRICK? YOU'LL GET PLENTY OF ATTENTION FROM THE AQUATIC POPULATION ONCE YOU'RE IN THE FUCKING SEA. MAYBE YOU'LL DRESS UP AS SPONGEBOB SQUAREPANTS FOR A WEEK IN THE HOPE THAT SOMEONE MIGHT LOOK AT YOU FOR A BIT. YOU FUCKING TWAT.

37 Gianmarco Tamberi

Using the de rigueur beard to draw attention isn't enough for Italian high jumper Tamberi. Oh no, he's up there with the king of the try-hards, because *his* beard only covers one side of his face.

That's right – like one of those performance artists that dresses up half and half as two different people and then proceeds to have an argument with themselves, Tamberi is part hipster, part clean-shaven, full dickhead.

Has he not got any mates? If he has, why the fuck haven't they staged some kind of intervention?

YOU DON'T EVEN DESERVE A FACE IF THAT'S THE BEST THING YOU CAN DO TO IT. GET IN THE FUCKING SEA, YOU APPALLING BEARD CRIMINAL.

36 Shingy

If you've never seen Shingy, you'll almost certainly piss yourself laughing when you do. Looking a bit like a cross between Gok Wan and the Goblin King out of *Labyrinth*, he's a so-called 'digital prophet'.

Impressive job description – he must be prophesying modern digital shizzle for some of the biggest names in the tech world, right? Actually, he works for AOL – the company that gave away millions of CD-ROMs in magazines two decades ago and who none of us have heard much from since. I'm sure they'll be back on top of the game once Shingy has prophesied some new stuff for them.

Not sure whether he's seaworthy yet? He also describes himself as 'an accidental singer-songwriter'.

FOR A PROPHET, YOU WEREN'T VERY GOOD AT PREDICTING YOUR SEA-BASED DEMISE, WERE YOU, YOU CHANCING LITTLE KNOBHEAD? GET IN THE FUCKING SEA.

35 Elizabeth Kesses

Describing herself as a 'writer, self-esteem advocate and ambassador for Dove', Elizabeth seems to have all the bases covered for a happy life. Especially the Dove stuff. Imagine how delectable your world would smell if you were an ambassador for a bar of soap.

In a recent interview, Elizabeth spoke passionately about her own personal sense of style, describing herself as an 'emotional dresser'. She said, 'Each morning, I ask myself how I want to feel. If I want to feel playful, I might choose my rainbow tank top. I love rainbows – they're all about hope and magic.'

Fuck off – rainbows are all about lies and leprechauns and shouting, 'It's there – above those trees on the left. Can't you see it? Look! LOOK!' at your children while you're trying to concentrate on driving.

MAYBE YOU CAN HUNT FOR RAINBOWS IN THE FUCKING SEA, ELIZABETH? OR BURIED TREASURE, OR MERMAIDS OR AQUATIC FUCKING UNICORNS.

34 Paul Weller

If you cut Weller in half, he'd have the word 'geezer' written all the way through him like Blackpool rock. As relentless as a Thursday, on and on he goes, churning out fifty-minute collections of the musical equivalent of a rump steak. Meaty, a bit dissatisfying, hard to swallow but nevertheless real. Not raw, and not well done either. Medium. No blood, though, or it's going back.

He's been doing this for over twenty years now – his combined spell as front man of The Jam *and* The Style Council (you know, the era when he was a bit decent) only lasted for eleven years or so.

Weller has become the music world's equivalent of a stuck record, but his fans are as much a part of the problem – an ageing crew of mods who are completely blind to the fact that the word derives from 'modernist' but yet continue to insist on dressing as if it's still 1967.

It's going to be unbearable when he dies, and for all the wrong reasons.

IT'S YOUR LEGION OF BELL END FANS THAT HAVE GOT YOU CONSIGNED TO THE DEEP, WELLER. BUT FUCK IT – YOU'VE DONE NOTHING TO DISCOURAGE THEM, SO IN YOU GO, YOU FUCKING MOD TOOL.

33 *Ricky Gervais*

We're only a decade and a half into the twenty-first century, but a hell of a lot has already happened. For example, it was way back in 2001 when *The Office* first appeared on TV, and Ricky Gervais was hailed by some as the future of British comedy.

Now? He's broken, a washed-up wreck, spending most of his time gibbering away on Twitter, wanging on endlessly about atheism and animal rights.

On the face of it, they sound like perfectly worthwhile, even noble causes, but his sanctimony becomes so cloying after a while that it can alter your mindset for the worse.

I recently read a whole month's worth of his pro-animal, anti-religion tweets and found myself compelled to go out, slaughter a badger and sacrifice it to the god I stopped believing in when I was seven years old.

Gervais' Twitter act almost makes you wish he'd be allowed to make more episodes of his fucking wretched *Derek* shitcom.

GET IN THE FUCKING SEA, YOU GRINNING, GURNING CUNT.

32 Donald Trump

This prick is almost to be admired for the way he's bulldozed his way through his entire life, giving it large with an expression on his face which suggests that nobody has ever said no to him before and, if they have, he's just ignored them and done whatever the fuck he liked anyway. But that's all there is to admire about him.

The truth is that he's a boorish, greedy, ignorant

arsehole and if he somehow manages to become the next President of the United States, you might as well get on the fucking bus to Dignitas, because it'll only be a matter of time before the planet is completely fucked and it won't be pretty.

YOU SHOULD HOPE THAT YOUR WEETABIX-STYLE HEAD-TOPPING DEVICE WILL HELP YOU TO FLOAT ONCE YOU'VE BEEN CONDEMNED TO THE FUCKING SEA FOR EVER MORE, YOU SHRILL, VACUOUS WASTE OF LUNGS AND BLOOD.

31 Rob Wilson MP

Your MPs are working for you, so it's important that you know exactly what they're up to and what they're spending your hard-earned tax cash on. Having said that, claiming 9p for a 352-yard car journey to a constituency event does look a bit parsimonious.

But that's Rob Wilson for you. The Tory MP for Reading East also once claimed 60p for a bicycle journey between his constituency office, the railway station and home. Hard to work out what there was about such a trip that he could claim for – wear and tear on his saddle, bike chain and the seat of his pants?

Closer inspection shows that, in the past five years, Wilson has made nearly 160 claims for travel expenditure that come in under £1.

He said that putting such small costs on expenses might seem 'odd', but said that over a year mileage 'does add up'. Mind you, it all seems like small beans compared to his £89,400 salary. The fucking tit.

DO YOU NOT EARN ENOUGH AS A TROUGH-SNUFFLING MP AS IT IS WITHOUT WAVING SHITE LIKE THIS IN THE FACES OF THE POOR FUCKERS (THE REST OF US) WHO HAVE TO FORK OUT FOR YOUR RIDICULOUS EXPENSES CLAIMS. TRY CLAIMING FOR A CAR JOURNEY ONCE YOU'RE IN THE FUCKING SEA AND SEE HOW FAR YOU GET, YOU RAGING ARSEHOLE.

Natural World

Pots of Shropshire air for sale

It's estimated (by me) that over £90 million is spent in the run-up to Christmas on novelty gifts – or to be more precise, shit made by cunts that is bought by other cunts to be given to different cunts because they don't have the imagination to be able to buy them a proper present.

Even though 71 per cent of the world is covered in water, there isn't enough sea for us to dispose of *all* of the shitty, unwanted novelty gifts, so we need to be selective. Chosen at random from a vast array of pointless fuckery comes the pot of Shropshire air.

I've been to Shropshire and can confirm that it's one of the most pointless parts of the United Kingdom. If England was a dog, Shropshire would be a piece of dried shit stuck to the fur around its arse.

As a county, when your largest settlement is fucking Telford, you know you're in serious trouble. If the Welsh ever decide to invade England, they'll go through Shropshire like a hot knife through butter, and the rest of us will be on the back foot.

All of which makes me wonder why anyone even half sane would want a pot of Shropshire air, unless they were going to use it as some kind of mild gateway before moving on to legal highs.

The pots, which are filled in a back garden in Bridgnorth before being heat-sealed, are priced at a quid a go on eBay. So it's not even pure air taken from a hilltop – it's infested by the stench of next door's wet washing and a whiff of the garden waste bin.

Rachel Moorcroft, the woman responsible for this, told the BBC: 'It's just a bit of fun.' Yes, Harold Shipman used to say that too. Probably.

IT'S EASY TO WRITE THIS SHIT OFF AS SOME WAG HAVING A BIT OF FUN BUT IF IT GETS OUT OF HAND YOU COULD BE LOOKING AT SOME MAJOR LEAGUE FRAUD. GET IN THE FUCKING SEA WITH YOUR POTS AND SEE HOW MANY YOU CAN FILL AS YOU STRUGGLE TO GET TO THE SURFACE.

That bloke who lived as a goat for a bit

We all have the urge to get away from it all from time to time, but for many of us a break from the norm consists of staying in all weekend with the curtains closed, accompanied by some box sets and Wotsits.

If you're a bit more adventurous, maybe you'll lock all the doors and treat yourself to a danger wank instead . . . but always be careful not to go Full Hutchence.

None of that is enough for designer Thomas Thwaites, though. He fancied turning his back on being a human, opting instead for the lifestyle of the humble goat. Sporting prosthetic limbs, Thwaites trip-trapped his way up the Swiss Alps and hung around with some goats in order to study their lifestyle. He even considered having a fake stomach fitted to let him eat grass. The fucking prick.

Other than the eating of grass and being up a hill, what the fuck else is there to learn about being a goat? And how much of a cunt did the other goats think he was? We can't read their minds or interpret their braying but my guess is 'a massive cunt'.

HEY, THWAITES – MAYBE AFTER YOU'VE FINISHED LIFE AS A GOAT YOU COULD TRY LIVING AS A FUCKING SEA HORSE FOR A WHILE? IN THE FUCKING SEA?

Dog shit etiquette

It's hard to believe now, but there used to be a time when it was pretty much okay for people to let their dogs shit all over the pavements. Or at least, if it was illegal, no one was enforcing it. Just like drink driving in the countryside – if you could manage to drive home through some winding narrow roads while you were pissed out of your head and still avoid ending up in a ditch, you were to be applauded.

But back to dog eggs. Because of the lackadaisical policing of them, the streets used to be awash with piles of shit, with kids wandering in off the street with it stuck to their shoes and sometimes on their hands and in their hair.

Things gradually changed, though, and nowadays, dog walkers head out armed with small plastic bags for gathering up their mutt's turds before they deposit the stinking placcy parcel in one of those special, shite-only bins that smell worse than Satan's dirty brother-in-law's arsehole after he's had a filthy night out on the beer and the curry.

Or at least, that's what the conscientious dog owners do. Some choose to be a bit more relaxed about the law, and they are the fuckers that will be going in the sea.

I've actually got a modicum of admiration for the people that don't bother cleaning up their dog's shit at all. They've drawn a line in the sand, and they've drawn it with some shit. 'Fuck your bags' is their message, and fair play to them.

What's worse is scooping your dog's dung up into the bag, tying the top, and then just leaving it on the ground. *Wankers.*

Better to hang the bag in a nearby tree like some other sociopathic dog owners do — hey, at least it's off the ground so no one can stand in it, and when there's a few of them hung there, they can look quite decorative, especially when the sunlight catches them.

SCOOP IT, BAG IT AND THEN BIN IT OR GET YOURSELVES IN THE FUCKING

SEA – RIGHT AT THE BIT WHERE THE SEW-
AGE PIPE PUMPS OUT HUMAN EFFLUENCE.

The Cecil the Lion Industry

In 2015, the world became as one, united in grief over the death of a beautiful and, more crucially, famous lion named Cecil, who hailed from South Africa or Zimbabwe or somewhere – that's not what's important.

What *is* important is that Cecil died for our sins, namely the sins of rich white men paying mahoosive sums of cash to shoot and kill mighty beasts while on safari in Kenya or Sri Lanka, or somewhere.

Okay, so Cecil wasn't actually famous here in the UK, but the news media told us that he was famous in his home land of Barbados or Uzbekistan or wherever, and that was kind of what sparked the global outrage and grief over his tragic, premature demise.

Shot dead in good faith (if that's possible under the circumstances) by an American dentist called Walter, Cecil became a cause célèbre across the globe for people who presumably were previously blissful in their ignorance about the existence of big game hunting.

Walter's dental surgery was picketed, and he disappeared from view for a while in case anyone took the lion law into their own hands and shot him too. Best of all, a mini Cecil industry sprung up as grabbing, chancing bastards tried to get on board and make the world look in their direction for fifteen seconds or so.

There were the psychic bell ends who claimed they had been in touch with Cecil's spirit and pronounced that he was happy in animal heaven, where he was presumably frolicking with Skippy the Bush Kangaroo, Wellard from *Eastenders* and maybe even Emu.

Animal psychic Karen Anderson even dictated a lengthy message from Cecil on her Facebook page. His words were:

> Let not the actions of these few men defeat us or allow darkness to enter our hearts. If we do then we become one of them. Raise your vibration and allow this energy to move us forward.
>
> What happened does not need to be discussed as it is what it is. Take heart my child, I am finer than ever, grander than before as no one can take our purity, our truth or our soul. Ever. I am here. Be strong and speak for all the others who suffer needlessly to satisfy human greed. Bring Light and Love and we will rise above this.

Yes, that sounds like what a lion might say as opposed to, perhaps, 'Where is meat?'

Then there were the left-field chancers, the ones you didn't really expect and couldn't help but admire. A company called Goldgenie hurriedly produced a gold-plated HTC One M9 mobile phone with a picture of dead Cecil engraved on the back, a snip at only £1,580, with 10 per cent going to a dead lion charity or something.

Cream of the crop though was the Sexy Cecil costume, pitched as a Halloween outfit, but hey, dressing as a sexy dead lion should be a 365-day-a-year thing, no? Mind you, you could also get a Walter the Dentist costume, which came with a severed lion head, so who's the real sicko, eh? Hmmm?

NONE OF YOU FUCKERS EVEN KNEW CECIL AND IF YOU'D MET HIM, HE'D PROBABLY TRY AND HAVE YOUR FUCKING LEG OFF BECAUSE HE WAS A FUCKING LION AND NOT SOME KIND OF OVERSIZED FAIRGROUND PRIZE. IN THE FUCKING SEA WITH THE LOT OF YOU.

Holistic dog food

Holistic: the belief that the parts of something are intimately interconnected and explicable only by reference to the whole.

Dog food: the brains, balls and bones of assorted animals that have been scraped off the floor of a slaughterhouse and fed into a machine in order to make some kind of vaguely edible meat pulp for canines.

Sorry, but I'm not feeling the connection here. Maybe the 'holistic' thing is a clever way of saying: 'Look, micro nutrients, yeah? Optimum nutritional value? M'kay?

'We've got something a bit different here and we're going to charge you five times the usual price for the privilege. Holistic – that word you've read in the *Guardian Weekend* magazine that makes you feel more reassured about stuff that might easily be just as shitty as the regular stuff you buy.

'Your dog might not like it at first but he'll get used to it after a few days because he's just a fucking dog and if he doesn't eat it he'll starve. Try not to focus on the price. Holistic.'

JUST FUCK OFF INTO THE FUCKING SEA WITH YOUR BULLSHIT DOG FOOD BEFORE I COME ROUND THERE AND RAM A BONE UP YOUR HOOP.

Sting's grape-picking scheme

It must be great being Sting. A dazzling career that spans almost forty years, with music, acting and that tantric sex stuff splattered all over his CV. He's renowned for his generosity of spirit too, having done charity work for UNICEF, Amnesty International and that tribal leader with a saucer for a tongue.

Sting's generosity has even extended to the grounds of his own home, inviting people in to share in his good fortune. If you wanted to visit his Tuscan estate in 2014, you could help pick grapes and olives and you'd get paid a handsome £208 for a day's labour. That's well above the minimum wage – Sting gets his fruit picked, you earn a few quid and get to hang out in the luxurious grounds belonging to your pop hero. Beautiful.

No, wait, what's this? Sorry, *you* would have had to

pay Sting £208 for the pleasure of picking his poxy grapes? What the actual fuck kind of scam is this?

You'd look to pay over half of that amount just to sit through one of his concerts, but would the 'entertainment' really be better or worse than eight hours of back-breaking labour in the Tuscany heat? Debatable, really.

The offer seems to have been subsequently withdrawn – maybe Sting is planning something new for his fans. £350 to suck barnacles off the hull of his yacht? A cool grand to get up his chimney with a brush attached to a top hat? How much to sit through a video of one of the aforementioned tantric sex sessions? The mind boggles.

GET IN THE FUCKING SEA, STING – I WOULDN'T PAY MONEY TO PISS ON YOU IF YOU WERE ON FIRE SO YOU CAN GO FUCK YOURSELF IF YOU THINK I'M DOING YOUR FUCKING GARDENING FOR YOU.

'Fur babies'

Pets are a great thing – they're cuddly, funny and . . . oh, other things that don't spring to mind right now. But please don't pretend that they're the equivalent of human offspring by referring to them as your 'fur babies'. Facebook, I'm looking specifically at you right now.

I'm sorry to break it to you, but if you own a cat, that cat does not give a flying fuck about you – it's living in your home solely because it finds it convenient right now.

If it gets a better offer (and you're lucky that it probably won't go looking for one), it'll be gone, and you'll have a bunch of spit-covered cat toys to chuck in the bin.

I'm sorry to break it to you, but if you own a dog, and you die suddenly, after a couple of days that dog will begin to feast on your corpse, starting with your eye-balls (as they are the juiciest bits of you).

All other domestic pets are too stupid to understand that you exist. They are not your fur babies – they are mistakes you have made.

IF YOU GENUINELY BELIEVE THAT THESE FLEA-RIDDLED CREATURES ARE YOUR BABIES THE ONLY WAY TO PROVE IT IS TO LET THEM SUCKLE ON YOU AND THEN POST PHOTOGRAPHIC EVIDENCE ON FACEBOOK. OTHERWISE YOU NEED TO GET IN THE FUCKING SEA.

Onesies on adults

Short of creating an actual massive replica of a fully operational womb, there's nothing that screams 'I can't adapt to modern life and I'd like to retreat back to from where I was originally hatched please' than the donning of a onesie.

We're only a couple of generations on from an era when adult men would be scandalized if they wore any-thing more casual than a shirt and tie around the house and yet we've somehow 'evolved' into a species that thinks nothing of lounging around dressed as a tiger while gawping at *The Great British Bake Off* and pushing Doritos through our face holes.

Worse still, there are people out there whose value systems are so crooked that they think popping out to the shops in their onesies is an okay thing to do. Should we be campaigning for a tweak in the law that would group public onesie-wearers in with dangerous animals such as the puma and the lynx, with a 'shoot on sight' policy when seen in public areas? I can't make a call like that, but I know that you're thinking about it right now and saying, 'Oooh, yes . . . ' to yourself.

IF THE ANIMAL LIFE APPEALS TO YOU SO MUCH, PERHAPS YOU SHOULD EAT OFF THE FLOOR AND SHIT OUTDOORS AND ROMP AROUND IN THE FUCKING SEA BEFORE SHAKING YOURSELF DRY IN THE BACK OF THE CAR.

Mars

Why the fuck are we all so obsessed with Mars and what may or may not be going on up there? We've all seen the footage from the probes that we've sent up – it's a fucking desert. Dry as sticks. Totally uninhabitable. A fucking write-off.

'But maybe we could colonize it,' bleat the more

excitable space fans. Yeah, maybe we could – but we'd all have to live inside temperature-controlled glass pods, owing to the ecosystem and lack of oxygen and all that. How about building your air-conditioned glass pods in the middle of the Sahara Desert instead? It looks a bit like Mars and, crucially, it's a fuckload nearer.

HOW ABOUT WE MAKE A MASSIVE NET, CATCH MARS IN IT AND THEN DROP IT IN THE FUCKING SEA? IT'S ABOUT AS PLAUSIBLE AS COLONIZING THE FUCKER.

Richard Branson's space fuckery

It must be fucking ace being Richard Branson. If he piled all his money up it would probably reach the Moon, but he still wants to do it the hard way by investing in a bunch of space planes, charging rich fuckwits a small fortune to fly up beyond the Earth's atmosphere, have a bit of a look about and then come down again.

No, wait, he's cracked it – he'll probably cream off enough profit from that to make his money pile tall enough to reach Mars. Hopefully he'll go on to colonize the mysterious red planet and do all the preparation for the first influx of migrants from down here. Virgin-branded houses, shops, bingo halls and suchlike – all ready for the lucky ones who have signed up to life on Mars.

Then, aside from the very, very rich, we'll be all like, 'Nah, don't fancy it any more. Go fuck yourself, pal.'

WHY NOT EXPLORE THE FUCKING SEA
INSTEAD – REBUILD ATLANTIS OR SOME-
THING. ANYTHING – JUST GET OUT OF
OUR FUCKING SIGHT FOR A BIT.

Three dead leaves for $19.99

Sure, it's your money and you can fritter it away on whatever you like, but when you're buying three dead leaves
direct from some twat in the USA for $19.99, there
should possibly be an intervention from social services,
for your own protection.

To be fair, the supplier, ShipFoliage.com, isn't trying
to pull a fast one or anything – they'll promise you three
colour-balanced leaves fresh from New England's most
beautiful trees: one red, one yellow and one green or
mixed. They're not trying to con you – being brazen
about the fact that they're charging you £13 plus shipping
for three fucking leaves is the genius of their scheme.

Still, though, fuck 'em.

GET IN THE FUCKING SEA, YOU PISS-
TAKING LEAF-BOTHERING FUCKERS.

Wasps

There's been a widespread campaign to save the bee in
recent years but it baffles me as to why all of that energy

couldn't instead be channelled towards the forced extinction of fucking wasps instead.

'Experts' will probably say that the eradication of an entire species would lead to the collapse of the ecosystem and an unpredictable, possibly apocalyptic future for the whole planet. You know what – I'll take my chances if it means I could have a pint in a beer garden in late August without being harangued by these stripy, arsey little cunts.

IF WE CAN'T KILL THE FUCKERS, ROUND THEM UP IN CONTAINERS IN THE HULL OF A SHIP, SAIL IT OUT INTO THE FUCKING SEA AND SINK IT.

Sport and Leisure

Fixed-odds betting machines

Venture into a bookies nowadays and you won't necessarily see what you'd expect. Sure, you'll find the sunken-eyed regulars who have semi-permanent residence there – men and women who have chewed the ends of so many tiny plastic pens that their colons are now hardened like the inside wall of the Channel Tunnel.

They're the old-school gamblers – the ones that have the occasional medium-sized win, which keeps them hopeful, nay *alive*, amid a relentless flurry of small, ego-battering losses.

These days, though, those people are there almost solely for decoration. The real action happens on the fixed-odds machines over in the corner. For the uninitiated, they're like the old one-armed bandits you used to get in pubs (remember pubs?) but they've been sprinkled with the same kind of fairy dust that makes crack cocaine a bit moreish.

The stakes are high on the fixed-odds machines, and if you're lucky you can win *big*. Chances are that you won't, though – you'll think you're going to, but just wind up jamming all of your food money for the next three weeks into the fucker.

For the bookies, these terminals are easy profit machines. For the problem gambler, they're worse than cancer. Of course, the bookies make all the right noises about responsible gambling and turn away punters who look like they've got a problem, but there's no shortage of fresh meat that will wander in off the street and chance their arm on their rotten machines.

STOP SUCKING THE HOPE, DREAMS AND CASH FROM PEOPLE WHO AREN'T STRONG ENOUGH TO WALK AWAY FROM YOUR SHITTY LURE AND GET IN THE FUCKING SEA.

Romeo Beckham's mascot gig

His shit name aside, Romeo Beckham must be one of the luckiest kids alive today. Raised by two parents who clearly adore him, it's safe to assume that he's insulated from many of the hardships that other children his age have to endure.

Good for him! No one wants to see any child endure a tough upbringing, and if Romeo gets to fly around the world, hang out with Pele and Robbie Williams and sit in the waiting room playing on a 128GB iPad while his dad gets a new tattoo, then fair play to him.

The problems begin, though, when we look at Romeo's recent thirteenth birthday gift: getting to lead out the England team at Wembley before their European Championship qualifier against Switzerland. Does he *really* need that experience to add to his life list? It's not as if he's sitting in the cheap seats at football matches, shivering his chin off, is it?

Afterwards, Romeo's dad admitted that the mascot thing had happened because he'd been able to use his influence at the FA. So, quite a few lessons for us all there.

Normal kids learn that the privileged classes will always get their own way, and that being on a waiting list could mean extra waiting while those in the know jump to the front of the queue.

We've also learned that David and Victoria Beckham haven't got the self-awareness to be able to either say to their kids that they have quite enough amazing stuff in their life and that being a mascot should perhaps be left for other kids, or that they're just pig ignorant.

Finally, we've learned that certain officials at the Football Association are just craven arselickers who will just ask, 'How high?' whenever David Beckham asks them to jump.

Yes, they're arguably the worst of the bunch, for not having the gall to follow the correct procedure and put Romeo on a waiting list.

STOP TOADYING TO THE RICH AND FAMOUS AND GIVE SOME OTHER POOR

LITTLE SOD A CHANCE, OR JUST GET IN THE FUCKING SEA.

Park-based exercise classes

We've all seen them – mobs of doughy, red-faced star-jumpers, huddled together in the corner of the local park. Frightened and panting, they hang on the every word of the barking arsehole who is both taking their money and getting to indulge in some kind of power trip by treating them like a pack of fresh squaddies forty-eight hours before a war is declared.

The cheapskate fucker in charge of this outdoor shit parade can't even go out of his way to find his hostages a venue with some warmth and shelter while they do all their unnatural gyrating and lunging, preferring instead to expose them to the elements and the mockery of bystanders, while he trousers an extra £30 towards a new set of stickers for the side of his 4x4, advertising his park fitness fuckery club.

For crying out loud, let them humiliate themselves and possibly die of a coronary in a nearby church hall instead, where there's toilets and privacy and no dog shit lying around for them to 'plank' in.

TRY DOING YOUR FUCKING STAR JUMPS ON THE OCEAN BED, EH? THERE'S NO FUCKING HIRE CHARGE DOWN THERE EITHER, YOU SKINFLINT FUCK.

Jogger's bells

There's few people more up their own arses than joggers, with all their specialist clothing and their overall sense of wellbeing and almost complete absence of obesity, shallow breathing and fear of climbing a staircase without stopping in the middle for a rest.

Except they don't call themselves joggers any more, because that implies a lack of speed. No, they're all runners, running around being fit and physically attractive but boring the living shit out of the rest of us when they post their running times and route maps on Facebook, or beg us for money because they're doing a 10k for Cat AIDS at the weekend. Fuck off, mate, no one's donating to my trifle fund, are they? And I'm calling you joggers right until the bitter end, when they turn off my life-support machine or when my furred arteries finally pack up for good.

The latest innovation that will almost certainly see some of these smug fuckers being dragged to the nearest coastal region and chucked into the sea is the jogger's bell. Just like a bicycle bell, the idea is that the jogger rings it when he's trotting down the pavement behind you, warning you that his important jogging is approaching your personal space and that you should get the fuck out of the way. That's because this self-absorbed prick doesn't have time to jog around you – he's coming through, and both you and your grab bag of Doritos could end up all over the deck if you're not careful.

If these jogger's bells become popular, they must surely serve as an indicator for the rest of us to stick out a leg and trip their diabolical users over as they go by.

THEY SAY THAT DOING GOOD JOGGING IS A CHALLENGE – SO IS SEEING HOW FAR UP AN ARSE A JOGGER'S BELL CAN BE SHOVED. GET IN THE FUCKING SEA WITH IT.

Booking fees

Word reaches you that your favourite singing artiste – let's say . . . Olly Murs – is coming to perform at your local aircraft-hangar-sized 'arena' venue – news that makes your shrivelled, barely functioning heart skip a beat.

Obviously, you don't want to miss out on this audio-visual extravaganza, you stupid twat, but you're worried that 15,999 other Murs customers will snap up a ticket before you do, so your gaze is fixed on a website and your fingers are poised as the tickets go on sale. After a worrying ten minutes in an online queue, hurrah – the tickets are in your online basket!

Okay, so they're a hundred metres back from the stage but there'll be big screens so it'll sort of feel like you're almost there. Just cough up your £63 and you're all sorted.

Hang on – didn't it say on the official Olly Murs dot-com that tickets would be £50 each? What fresh hell is this? That's your booking fees – or scum tax if you'd prefer a snappier name for them.

For years now, we've been sleepwalking into this shithousery, buying our tickets and barely batting an eyelid as the vendor adds another 15 per cent on top seemingly for the sheer hell of it.

The best ones are those that charge you £2.50 to print your ticket out at home. What the fucking fuck? Two pound fifty when there's absolutely no postage or packaging involved? No human interaction whatsoever, just a second-long whirr on a computer database as the transaction is completed?

Two pound fifty for the privilege of doing your fucking ticket at home, on your crappy little printer? Have you seen the fucking price of ink these days?

STOP FLEECING US WITH YOUR ROBBING FUCKING BOOKING FEES AND GET IN THE FUCKING SEA. IT'S BAD ENOUGH THAT WE'RE MAKING TERRIBLE LIFE DECISIONS SUCH AS PROPPING UP THE SHOWBIZ EMPIRES OF THE LIKES OF OLLY MURS WITHOUT YOU CUNTS TAKING THE PISS AS WELL.

Hardcore cyclists

I'm not talking about the ones who pootle around the UK's admirable cycle network or the ones that do a coast-to-coast in three days to raise money for animal cancer – it's the shouty, militant fuckers that are the problem. The ones that are half man (because they're almost always men), half bike, and are so lean from their constant cycling that their Lycra looks practically sprayed on.

You've seen him – he's the sort that never goes anywhere without a GoPro camera screwed into the top of his skull so that he can upload on to YouTube footage of a taxi driver calling him a cunt, which will then go viral and get the taxi driver sacked and his life ruined when in fact he was making a perfectly valid point about the cyclist cunt who cut him up half a mile back.

He's the sort that will take to Twitter to defend anyone against any kind of anti-cyclist comment, regardless of whether he follows them or not. He's probably got a list of automatic key word searches on there to help him, like 'jumped a red light', 'riding on the pavement' and 'almost killed a kid when he rode straight through a zebra crossing'.

He'll wade in with a 'not all cyclists' defence, while blaming everyone from the police to traffic wardens to 1970s town planners. Everyone except the prick who jumped the red light and almost killed the kid, an incident which, of course, the hardcore cyclist didn't even see.

SEE IF YOU CAN PEDAL YOUR WAY OUT OF THE MURKY DEPTHS OF THE FUCK-ING SEA, YOU TWISTY PRICK.

Sky Sports News' Football Manager obsession

Running a rolling sports news TV channel is a fucking ludicrous way of conducting yourself. There just isn't enough noteworthy stuff happening at any given time to justify endless hours of previews, opinions and highlight clips that are pumped into our eyeballs around the fucking clock. And yet Sky Sports News has been doing it for years.

Recently, though, they've started almost taking the piss out of us, by using stats from the Football Manager computer game when discussing players' strengths and weaknesses. Don't get me wrong, it's a brilliant game, and I'm sure there's a lot of dedicated researchers out there collating these figures about players' attributes, but . . . but . . . fuck off, eh?

PUT YOUR COMPUTER GAMES IN THE FUCKING SEA AND DO SOME PROPER JOURNALISM INSTEAD. THIS IS LIKE SKY NEWS USING CALL OF DUTY ON THE

XBOX AS A REPLACEMENT FOR A REPORT FROM A WAR ZONE. OH FUCK, THEY'LL PROBABLY DO THAT NEXT.

Smug rugby fans

Whenever there's a controversy in football, there's always a rugby fan nearby, tutting, shaking his head and saying, 'You'd never see that happen in our game'. He is, without exception, an utter twat.

Footage of pissed-up football fans running amok in some European city? Up pops the rugby fan, blathering on about how fans of *his* sport can drink beer in their seats while watching a match and not get into a fight. That'll be because rugby is a sport for emotionally stunted middle-aged men who are unable to articulate their feelings about anything and just sit there, politely waiting to die.

Footballers caught on camera deliberately diving or play-acting? 'It'd never happen in our sport,' says the rugby fan, wanging on about 'real men' while striving for the moral high ground and simultaneously being unable to cry, ever.

Of course, he'll forget about all the punching, biting, and gouging that happens in his precious sport, not to mention the 'Bloodgate' episode when a fake blood capsule from a Clapham joke shop was used in a match in order to gain a tactical advantage, only to spectacularly backfire.

Yeah, yeah – superior game. Course it is. Fuck off back to your emotional repression and your egg chasing.

GET IN THE FUCKING SEA WITH YOUR WEIRDLY SHAPED BALLS AND YOUR ABJECT FEAR OF EMOTIONS.

Dog yoga

Dogs don't want to do fucking yoga – they want to lick their balls, sniff the arseholes of other dogs, eject feeble jets of piss in sixteen locations during a twenty-minute walk and chew a pig's ear in front of the fire. For the average dog, anything else is a bit of a stretch.

Sadly for our canine pals, some humans reckon they know better and have decided that dog yoga, or 'doga' as the fuckers are calling it, is just what the world needs.

According to the leading 'Dogmahny' (no, no idea why it's called that) website, 'having your dog included in your yoga practice enables you to observe "your attitude" towards yourself and all living beings and get a deeper insight and understanding of behaviour patterns that arise from the mind'.

Presumably it also enables your agitation levels to soar as you try and get your unwilling mutt to hold a series of yoga poses with you when all it really wants to do is get its tummy tickled or chase a stick.

WHY THE FUCK DO YOU HATE YOUR DOG SO MUCH TO INVOLVE IT IN YOGA? FOCUS ON THE FACT THAT IT'S YOURSELF THAT YOU HATE AND KEEP THE POOR POOCHES OUT OF IT OR GET IN THE FUCKING SEA.

Pushchairs for dogs

For dogs, now is comfortably the worst time to be alive. Humanity's incessant need to fuck about with stuff that doesn't need to be fucked with has led us first to dog yoga and now this, the dog pushchair.

Yes or no – does your dog enjoy, and is it able to do, exercise? If yes, you don't need a pushchair for the fucker, as it should be pegging it all over the place using its tried and trusted quadruped running system.

If no, just leave it in the house so it can lie around – it's clearly old or knackered and just wants to be left alone as opposed to being wheeled around fucking Argos in the afternoons.

Your dog is not a baby – if you can't have a baby, you have my sympathy, but stop trying to replicate the experience with a helpless hound. You'll be trying to sign it up for the local primary school next and threatening the council with the international court of human rights when they send back your application cut up into little bits.

IT'S YOU THAT BELONGS IN A PUSH-CHAIR – STRAPPED IN TIGHTLY AND THEN PUSHED OVER THE EDGE OF A CLIFF STRAIGHT INTO THE FUCKING SEA.

People who don't like sport

Never trust a man whose eyes are close together, or so they say. But what constitutes 'close together'? Do we need to be equipped with some kind of eyeball gauge, so that we can make an accurate assessment before befriending someone new?

No, simply ask them what their favourite sport is, and you'll soon find out if they're one of the good guys or not. Chances are they'll say 'football' or 'darts' or 'tennis', and you know you're on safe territory.

But if they screw their face up a bit and say, 'You know, I'm not really a fan of sport. I'm not into that competitive kind of thing – I've never understood the appeal,' you need to give them the same kind of wide berth that you'd dish out to a convicted arsonist or a 1970s TV presenter.

Give these fuckers an inch and they'll take a mile. Never mind about the distance between their eyes, they'll soon be up to all sorts, from talking about you behind your back to undermining you in the workplace. Spend any length of time with a non-sport-lover and I guarantee you they'll be stealing your identity and syphoning your savings into an untouchable Cayman Islands account.

Even rugby fans are better than people who don't like any sport at all – and rugby fans are utter scum.

YOU CAN START YOUR SPORTING EDUCATION BY GETTING IN THE FUCKING SEA AND PLAYING WATER POLO WITH THE SHARKS, YOU SLIPPERY WANKERS.

The price of vinyl

It's nice that vinyl is still around – it's reassuring that modern technology hasn't been able to kill off something that has meant so much to generations of music lovers. But fuck me rigid with a hot tablespoon, have you seen the price of it these days?

You can pick up a triple CD of Motown classics for about a fiver in any decent supermarket but try to get the new album by Pink Floyd frontman David Gilmour on vinyl and you'll be shelling out the thick end of £25. It's illogical – not least because Motown is aural nectar and Pink Floyd are the musical equivalent of being stuck in a revolving door full of bees.

You can't even cheat and pick up some old vinyl on the cheap from your local charity shop any more. They all must have some kind of discography expert sat in the back room on a small mountain of dead men's cardigans, analysing each and every record that is donated and pricing the lot just above what the standard skinflint would be prepared to pay.

£4.99 for *Bangs and Crashes* by Go West? Go fuck yourself, British Heart Foundation.

YOU CAN STICK YOUR FUCKING VINYL IN THE SEA – I'M ILLEGALLY DOWN-LOADING EVERY SINGLE ALBUM EVER RELEASED AND PUTTING IT ALL ON A HARD DRIVE THE SIZE OF A CARAVAN, ALL OUT OF PURE SPITE.

Festival glamping

Surely the whole point of going to a music festival is to temporarily wave goodbye to your pampered lifestyle and embrace the kind of living hell that was endured by our forefathers as they fought in the trenches in the First World War.

Mud, disease, stray dogs, food poisoning, cunts with bongos – they're all part of what makes the festival experience so unique, and that's before you factor in watching Coldplay while standing a quarter of a mile from the stage, pissed up on warm lager and wishing you were at home.

The great leveller for everyone at a festival is the accommodation. On the whole, it's tents, and if you're a bit flash, you'll sleep in a camper van. Increasingly, though, the sordid, middle-class world of glamping has infested the festival scene. You can now pay way over the odds and kip in a wigwam, a bell tent or a yurt – the camping equivalent of a VIP section in a nightclub.

Some of these plainly wrong upscaled options even come with electricity, access to VIP showers and, for all I know, special receptacles for wanking into when you get overly excited about how you're better than everyone else because you're dossing in a yurt while everyone else is knee-deep in their own shite and trying to escape the Nostalgia Field before fucking Marillion come on.

WHAT THE FUCK IS A BELL TENT ANYWAY? IT'S A TENT FOR FUCKING BELL ENDS AND IT BELONGS IN THE FUCKING SEA.

Transfer Deadline Day

Twice a year, football flies right up its own arsehole, leaving behind a vapour trail of hyperbole, disappointment and rank stupidity. Yes, it's Transfer Deadline Day – clubs' last opportunity to buy and sell players for a few months.

Essentially it's their last chance to flog off some of the

bone-idle wankers that have been syphoning money from their coffers and enraging supporters with their ineptitude, or maybe bringing in some new players that will subsequently go on to syphon money from their coffers and enrage supporters with their ineptitude.

Football – it's all about opinions, but one thing that's a given is that 95 per cent of your team's players will get right on your fucking tits at some point during their time at your beloved club.

We've got Sky Sports News to thank for making Transfer Deadline Day into the circus of piss and wind that it has become. Their coverage in the days, nay weeks, leading up to it has become increasingly ludicrous, their correspondents jizzing out rumours and half-truths around the clock, all the while adding up exactly how many squillions of quids have been spunked by clueless, desperate football club owners as they aim to avoid relegation, humiliation, bankruptcy or maybe all three.

None of it as humiliating as Sky Sports News' pride in their 'ingest area' though – their bank of TV screens and various video feeds from around the country, with trained operators ready to break the news when Rotherham United spend £300,000 on a new left back or when a nineteen-year-old millionaire from Chelsea's reserves goes out on loan to Anderlecht.

In spite of all the hype, that's usually as exciting as it gets on Deadline Day – the old-style flurry of last-minute transfers doesn't happen quite so much any more, with increasingly canny clubs looking to get the right deals done with time to spare.

So we're left to stare at Jim White mangling his words and trying to ramp up the excitement levels as the clock ticks down and fuck all actually happens. But who's the real arsehole – him, or us for sitting through it time after time?

It's not even as much fun as it used to be – in the past, Sky's reporters would appear outside various club's grounds, accompanied by local reprobates, whooping and hollering incessantly while no doubt high as kites on hippy crack (the locals, not the reporters). This uneasy alliance came to an end when reporter Alan Irwin had a blue dildo rammed into his earhole at Everton, and reporters now broadcast from a safe place, free of interlopers.

GET IN THE FUCKING SEA AND SEE HOW INTERESTED WE ALL ARE IN THE LAST-MINUTE TRADING OF FUCKING STARFISH AND FUCKING COD AND THAT.

Fireworks

Fireworks used to be great back when cars couldn't go faster than 65 mph and there were only three channels on the telly to choose from. Now though, we've got 86,000 channels, and Grand Theft Auto –

but fireworks are still the same as they were thirty years ago.

Stop dragging your kids along to organized firework displays – you're boring the shit out of them, and the money raised is probably going towards the continuation of the freemasons anyway.

Worse still are supermarket fireworks – fifty quid for a few pops, bangs and colourful crackles that underwhelm everyone that sees and hears them while agitating every animal within a 500-yard radius. You pointless, money-spunking cunts.

FUCK OFF INTO THE SEA, FIREWORKS, WHERE YOU'LL BE RENDERED UNUSABLE FOR EVER.

Quidditch World Cup

If the raging success of the Harry Potter books and films has taught us anything it's that adult humans need very little encouragement when it comes to embracing their inner child. Special 'adult' versions of the Potter books were a raging success when they were published, allowing grown-ups to pretend that they weren't in fact reading children's books in public, slightly lowering their raging levels of self-loathing a bit.

For some of these infantalized wanksocks, Potter has become a way of life, and the fictional sport of

Quidditch, which looms large in the made-up children's stories, has grabbed their imaginations so much that they've started playing it themselves and even staging a global tournament.

Small point of detail though – in the books, Quidditch is played on broomsticks, with competitors whizzing around in the sky. Here in the real world, the participants run around a boggy field with broomsticks between their legs. You know, just like when a seven-year-old pretends to be riding a horse.

Broomsticks. Between their legs. Actual adults.

GET IN THE FUCKING SEA WITH YOUR PRETEND SHITHOUSE SPORTS DAY.

Half and half scarves

The number one scourge of modern football – match-specific knitwear with a half dedicated to each of the two competing teams. Do you know anyone who has forked out for one of these monstrosities? What even possesses someone to consider such a piece of utter, utter fuckery.

Fan of Sunderland are you? Why not trample all over that loyalty by donning a half and half Sunderland/ Norwich scarf when the Canaries come to town? That yellow and green will look beautiful next to your team's red and white.

And when will you wear it again? Yes – when hell freezes over. You calamitous tosspot.

GOT ONE OF THESE? YOU SHOULD BE HURLED INTO THE FUCKING SEA USING A CATAPULT MADE FROM A BUNCH OF THEM TIED TOGETHER.

Disneyland Paris

If you're the parent of a young child, this continental pleasure park sounds good in theory, but if you go when it's cold and damp you're going to need at least a couple of months of counselling once you get home.

If you saw Banksy's Dismaland theme park exhibition thing in 2015 and have ever been to Disneyland Paris in October, you'll be genuinely stuck over which one seems like the best prospect for a return visit.

Teeming with pig-ignorant bundesfuckers who don't know what a queue is or does, EuroMausLand will clean out your pockets while making you feel a bit grubby in as little as forty-eight hours. There's a reason why scores of Syrian refugees prefer to hang out in a squalid camp in Calais rather than stop off at Disneyland Paris for a day on their way to Britain. They might be desperate but they're not fucking stupid.

Don't go – I implore you. Commit an armed robbery and use the proceeds to head for Florida instead. If you can get away with it, fantastic – if not, five years behind bars will still be better than a week at Disneyland Paris.

THIS NOXIOUS IMITATION OF HIGH-GRADE FLORIDA FAMILY FUN NEEDS TO BE WINCHED UP BY A HELICOPTER AND DROPPED RIGHT INTO THE FUCKING SEA.

Earth's Fifty Worst Humans: Part 3

30 Juris Dzjabovic

Part of me admires this fucker, who charged a whopping £206 fare to a family after taking them on a mile-long ride on his rickshaw from Oxford Circus to Marble Arch. The sheer gall of that fare is truly a thing of wonder and beauty.

After all, as Dzjabovic himself said in his defence, he had to pedal uphill. 'I don't come cheap,' the Moscow-born opera singer said. 'I work my legs hard, I look good and I play good music – you have to pay a lot if you want that kind of luxury.'

Okay, so he might have started to get into the mindset of a high-class hooker a little bit there but he takes pride in his work, so why shouldn't he charge top dollar?

In fact, he went on to argue that he was offering them a discount. Dzjabovic later told the *Mail*, 'I charged £206 because there were four people and I was going uphill. I didn't even charge them the full amount – it should have been £412.'

You've got to admire his brass neck but ultimately, no. No fucking way.

THERE'LL BE NO SHORTAGE OF VOLUN-
TEERS TO TIE THIS GRABBING WANKER
TO THE BACK OF HIS RICKSHAW AND
DRAG IT ALL THE WAY TO THE FUCK-
ING COAST BEFORE LIFTING IT HIGH
ABOVE THEIR HEADS AND HURLING IT
AND HIM OFF THE EDGE OF A CLIFF,
STRAIGHT INTO THE FUCKING SEA. THE
CUNT.

29 Ryan Adams

This dull, hairy indie rocker has been the critics' favourite since what feels like 1977 even though there's more
tunes on one side of a single by his near-namesake Bryan
than in the whole of Ryan's back catalogue.

His most recent statement was to take Taylor Swift's
sparkling, gleaming and glorious *1989* album and reinter-
pret it in his own image. It was about as blatant and ugly
an example of musical 'mansplaining' as you'll ever
encounter.

'Okay, little lady – you've made your bubblegum
pop album, and millions of people have gone out and
bought it, but here's *my* take on it – here's how it sounds
when it's done by a "real" musician.' The cheeky fucking
twat.

I've heard it – compared to Taylor Swift's version, it's
utter dog shit. As you'd expect.

OFF YOU FUCK INTO THE SEA YOU
TIRED, MIDDLE-AGED KNACKER.

28 Dapper Laughs

This persistent bell end made his name as one of the
pioneers of the six-second Vine video format (if
you've never heard of it or indeed him, you're missing
nothing) but more recently has been seen trying to sal-
vage the paltry excuse for a career that he previously
had.

It's all about bantz for the lads with Dapper – cheeky
quips at the birds, tongue-in-cheek offers of casual sex
and the occasional rape joke just when things aren't feeling sour enough.

His shtick was lambasted online and in the press in
2014 but like some kind of comedy cockroach, he seems
to be unbreakable, coming back again and again, blaming everyone but himself for his woes while appealing to
an increasingly dwindling audience.

With a face like the swept-up contents of an abattoir floor and a personality that is as appealing as
cholera, it's a wonder that anyone has ever managed to
stomach more than six seconds of this abominable
prick.

WE JUST NEED ONE MORE SIX-SECOND
VIDEO FROM YOU, LAUGHS – OF YOU
BEING TOSSED INTO THE FUCKING SEA.

27 *Daft As Punk*

There's a Daft Punk tribute group out there. Just how fucking hard can that really be? Step one: put on Daft Punk-esque headgear that you've made yourself out of a couple of motorbike crash helmets and some silver foil. Step two: put on a tape of Daft Punk's greatest hits.

STEP THREE: GET IN THE FUCKING SEA, YOU LAZY, CONNIVING SHITHEADS.

26 *Nick Grimshaw*

In years to come, when they ask what caused *The X Factor* to finally wither and die, those of us who remember it all will stare into the middle distance and mutter, 'Nick fucking Grimshaw.'

He's still in work at the moment, but future generations will look back and see that this irritating, braying shit wizard was actually the broadcasting version of the Ebola virus, decimating audience figures wherever he pitched up.

Since he landed the Radio 1 breakfast show, 'Grimmy' has lost about one million listeners while at least two million *X Factor* viewers have given him the once over and gone, 'Fuck *that*' before switching off for ever.

There's still a lot of work for Grimshaw to do, though – weirdly, large swathes of the population haven't yet realized just how fucking intolerable his banter is and appear to be content with having his face and voice pushed into their brains on a regular basis. They'll learn . . .

HERE'S WHAT'LL BOOST YOUR RATINGS – YOU DOING THE RADIO 1 BREAKFAST SHOW FROM THE MURKY DEPTHS OF THE OCEAN AFTER YOU'VE BEEN CATA- PULTED IN THERE FOR YOUR CRIMES AGAINST LISTENING. IN YOU FUCKING GO.

25 *Noel Edmonds*

The telly and radio veteran isn't shy when it comes to dreaming up random and unlikely theories about life, the universe and all that bollocks. And don't forget that he came up with Mr Blobby, so we're clearly dealing with a deep thinker here.

But there's way more to Noel than hosting *Deal Or No Deal* for ever or until the Earth spins off its axis and collides with the Sun. Oh, and the ever-darkening of his tidy beard while the rest of him seems to have defied the ageing process. Way way more than all that.

One of his most recent public thoughtfarts was about 'electrosmog' – clouds of electromagnetic fields caused by wi-fi, phone signals and electricity. It's endangering humanity apparently, making us electrosensitive (oooh, can you feel the chill?), and systematically destroying our own natural electromagnetic fields.

That'll explain why I've been feeling grumpier in the mornings and why my piss doesn't shoot out with the same ferocity as it used to. It'll be the electrosmog.

Try and think of it as being like a cyber version of carbon monoxide – the only subtle difference being that carbon monoxide is a scientifically recognized killer and that electrosmog is a load of old shit dreamed up by the bloke who used to drop gunge on Tony Blackburn's head on BBC1 on a Saturday evening.

ELECTROSMOG WON'T BE AN ISSUE ONCE YOU'VE BEEN CONDEMNED TO THE DARKENED DEPTHS OF THE FUCKING SEA, YOU WEIRD BASTARD.

24 Bhanu Prakash

Bhanu used to hold down a pretty decent job, as a pharmaceutical research assistant in Hyderabad, India, but in the summer of 2015 he sacked it all off to follow his dream – namely to break the world record for the number of selfies taken in an hour.

He gave up his job? Did he not realize that this grand project of his would only take him sixty minutes? Sure, there's some practising involved, but a couple of hours in the evenings would quickly bring him up to speed.

It's obvious what's happened here – Bhanu has been

sacked from the pharmaceutical research gig (probably for pissing about and taking selfies when he should be researching all those pharmaceuticals) and, rather than fess up to his wife, he's trying to style it all out by casting himself as a hero for the modern age; a pioneer in narcissism and rapid button pushing.

Weirdly, since Bhanu announced his bold record attempt, not a single thing has been heard from him. He probably found another job and is trying to pretend that none of it ever happened.

GET IN THE FUCKING SEA, YOU BLUFFING, MOBILE-WIELDING BELL END.

23 Britain First

One of the most wearying feelings imaginable is when someone you care about shares a post by these absolute fuckers on Facebook. Of course, it won't be one of their far right, outright racist ones. No, it'll be one of the ones showing an emaciated spaniel, with 'click like if you think being bad to animals is bad' next to a Paypal donation link. Or one of the ones that uses Lee Rigby's name and image to further their bullshit ideology, in contravention of the wishes of Lee's family.

That's what these shitheels do — paint themselves as the purveyors of all that is right and good and then slip in some Islamophobia or benefit bashing when you're not expecting it. They're not a genuinely powerful political force, but with almost a million people on Facebook following their page, they're getting dangerously close.

There's still a strong element of secrecy about them, though. If you fancied going to their last annual party conference, the Days Inn hotel at the Welcome Break services in Sheffield was the place to be . . . at first. According to their Facebook page, once you arrived there, 'you will be handed the final re-direction point'.

Like an acid house rave, but with barmy far right hectoring at the secret location instead of beats and drugs.

THESE FUCKERS' FINAL RE-DIRECTION POINT SHOULD BE OFF THE SACRED WHITE CLIFFS OF DOVER AND STRAIGHT INTO THE FUCKING SEA.

22 *The Stone Roses*

They're back again – looking increasingly like four terminally ill blokes who spend their disability allowance money on motorbike restoration while wondering which will be the next one to shit himself.

Having made no new music whatsoever since 1994, these days the group exists solely as a masturbatory aid for men in their forties who are weeping at the loss of their youth, giving them an excuse to fill a football stadium every few years, make complete tits of themselves on mind-spinningly expensive but piss-weak lager.

A QUARTET OF DECENT SONGS AND
SOME MEMORIES OF SUN HATS AND
CHEAP ECSTASY ISN'T ENOUGH TO KEEP
YOU OUT OF THE FUCKING SEA.

21 *Kirstie Allsopp*

This daughter of a baron seemed quite harmless during
the 692 series of *Location Location Location Location Location*
on Channel 4, but if you've encountered her on
Twitter, you'll know that she's actually a spiteful, judg-
mental Tory witch.

Allsopp recently threw a Twitter strop about students
who were protesting against tuition fees, which is all
well and good when you left school at seventeen and
wandered into a series of jobs working for your parents.
Fuck everyone else that might not have access to that
kind of privilege and fuck their aspirations.

LOCATION LOCATION LOCATION AT THE
BOTTOM OF THE FUCKING SEA.

Food and Drink

Crisp sandwich shop

If you're after a quick, tasty lunch or something to fill your face once you get in from the pub, you can't beat a crisp sandwich. Ready in under half a minute, it's the chip butty for the lazy and the desperate.

But if someone wandered up to you in the street and announced that they'd make you a crisp sandwich but that they'd want paying for it, you'd be perfectly within your rights to spin them around and kick them repeatedly up the arse until you reached the edge of town.

While no one was really surprised that a crisp sandwich shop opened in 2015, you'd expect it to be based in London's wanker hub of Shoreditch, knocking out a handful of Walkers jammed between two slices of medium white for a fiver a pop.

No – the aptly named 'Mr Crisp' is in Keighley. In West Yorkshire. In the North. Where you'd think they'd know better.

'I have always had an idea to open a crisp sandwich shop,' said proprietor Mark Pearson, immediately striking fear into our hearts as we realize that he's actually been letting this plan ferment for a number of years, instead of it being a desperate last-ditch attempt at fending off financial ruin.

'I could either sit on the fence and get left behind or go and take a chance,' he said, speaking of his life-altering decision.

Yeah, mate – good for you, sticking your neck out and giving the world something that it didn't even know it needed. They'll look back at you as some kind of culinary pioneer and there'll be a crisp sandwich shop on every high street in Britain.

As this book went to press, no other crisp sandwich shops had opened in Britain. Early days though.

SERIOUSLY, THOUGH, ANY FUCKER WITH HALF A BRAIN AND AS FEW AS THREE FINGERS CAN KNOCK OUT A CRISP SANDWICH WITHOUT HAVING TO VISIT SOME KIND OF HALF-BAKED EXCUSE FOR A SHOP FOR ONE. THIS WEAK, EXPLOITATIVE SHITE BELONGS IN THE FUCKING SEA.

Monty Bojangles Choccy Scoffy

There's a reason why wandering around shops while brandishing a baseball bat is generally frowned upon – it's because the retailers know that they're pedalling more and more shite that might provoke us into wielding said sports weapons in a violent and unwanted manner.

And if you don't believe me, *you* try mooching around your local mall while menacingly twirling a bat like a deranged majorette – trust me, you won't last long.

Anyway, witness these cocoa-dusted truffles – definitely available in Waitrose but less likely to be found up the Asda. They probably taste delicious, but I'll never know, because the potential shame that could come from being spotted with them more than outweighs the taste benefits.

Hello, here's Monty Bojangles himself (or rather, some dizzy PR copywriting cunt), and he says: 'I found these gloriously indulgent utterly chocolatey cocoa-dusted truffles whilst trundling through a marvellously magnificent land of prettily pink flamingoes on my simply super jalopy. They are so curiously moreish and scrumptiously scoffable I decided to call them Choccy Scoffy. You really have to try them! For the giddily curious discover the rest of our range at montybojangles. com.'

Now you understand what I meant about the bat, don't you?

THIS PISSY-MISSY, SHITTY-TITTY, BELL-ENDY-WENDY INFANTALIZATIONY-WAT-IONY TWEENESS BELONGS IN AMONG THE TURBULENCE OF THE WAVES AND NOT ON THE SHELVES OF OUR SHOPS.

One of the few things in life that remains unfucked with by hipsters and chancers is the cooked breakfast. A design classic like motorway road signs and the felt-tip pen, you can't piss about with sausages, bacon, egg, tomato and mushrooms.

Baked beans, though? Are beans an interloper or do they belong in the breakfast line-up? That's a different debate for a different day.

But if we accept that beans belong in the cooked breakfast (and let's not start mulling over hash browns or even . . . chips), surely they have to be allowed to take equal standing on the plate. This bullshit where they get served up separately in a ramekin can't be allowed to flourish, can it?

It's the thin end of the wedge – they'll be scattering herbs all over the fried egg next. No. No. No.

TO DENY BEANS THEIR FREEDOM TO OOZE AND ROAM AROUND ON A PLATE IS TO DENY THEIR VERY EXISTENCE. THE RAMEKIN IS A BEAN PRISON AND BELONGS IN THE DEPTHS OF THE FUCK-ING SEA.

Mini burgers

Some things just aren't intended to be enjoyed in small doses – I'm thinking cheesecake, continental-strength lager and daydreams about tying George Osborne to a pole and flogging him to within an inch of his life.

You can add burgers to the list as well. The humble burger has been hijacked by the forces of darkness that want to take everything we love and fuck about with it for no decent reason.

Mini burgers are the disgusting pinnacle of this – the modern day vol-au-vent that no one actually wants. More and more buffets everywhere are being fucked up beyond recognition by this atrocity – one mini burger is never going to be enough, and twenty-seven might just be too many.

In fact, the miniaturization business as a whole needs to be put a stop to – tiny bottles of wine aimed at people who don't have the willpower to stop guzzling the stuff after one glass are a major worry (although admittedly they're nice to enjoy during a toilet break at work).

FOR FUCK'S SAKE, JUST PUT SOME PROPER BURGERS OUT AND LET US WOLF THEM LIKE THE SAVAGES WE ARE, INSTEAD OF TANTALIZING US WITH TINY VERSIONS. THIS ISN'T LILLIPUT, YOU FUCKERS – NOW GET IN THE FUCKING SEA.

The Tomami burger

Or as it's better known, 'that fucking burger with a tomato for a bun' – a culinary atrocity that quite possibly sits at the very epicentre of the whole 'fucking about with perfectly good food for no real reason' movement that has blighted the world in recent years.

In case you're not familiar with it, it hails from the Japanese MOS Burger chain and is a standard burger that sits betwixt a massive tomato that has been sliced in half. It was launched as a strictly limited edition, which is always the best method to deploy if you want to convince utter pricks that the total shit you're flogging is in any way desirable.

The Tomami's closest cousin is KFC's Double Down, a 'sandwich' that is comprised of bacon, two different kinds of melted cheese, the Colonel's secret sauce . . . all housed in between two pieces of Original Recipe chicken fillets. You have to admire the Double Down, though – it's not trying to push any health agenda like the Tomami. The Double Down doesn't care if you die or not, so you might as well just get stuck in.

On similar territory is American chef Tommy Updegrove, who brought his nonsense burger range to the UK in 2015. Among the attention-seeking shite he's punting is a 1,400 calorie burger topped with a Philly cheese steak encased in a halved and glazed doughnut, and a chicken burger with a 'bun' made from Coco Pops.

He should have been subjected to some kind of

detailed personality test before he was allowed in the country. He would surely have failed it.

STOP FUCKING ABOUT WITH BURGERS AND BUNS AND ALL THAT IS HOLY WHEN IT COMES TO FAST FOOD. A TOMATO IS NOT A BUN IN THE SAME WAY THAT SALT IS NOT SUGAR. JUST FUCKING LEAVE IT ALONE OR GET IN THE FUCKING SEA.

The M&S Yorkshire pudding sandwich

The twenty-first century's greatest collective delusion is that nothing we already have is satisfactory and that there must be an endless search to do things in a new and quirky way.

Our ancestors weren't bothered about new or quirky – their main concerns were things like not freezing to death or being eaten by a mammoth or falling foul of an agonizing industrial injury. We've got lazy and complacent and let our guard down and allowed Marks and Spencer to do sandwiches with roast beef and Yorkshire pudding in them, and we've gone too far and we should probably consider global nuclear suicide and let whatever survives take our place and try to do things better.

If I was a betting man, I'd be prepared to put serious money on Humanity 2.0 not fucking about by putting Yorkshire puddings in sandwiches. Chances are that I wouldn't be around to collect my winnings, though, and who's to say that gambling would continue to exist?

This has all gone a bit grim – see what you've done, M&S??

A YORKSHIRE PUDDING DOES NOT GO IN A SANDWICH IN THE SAME WAY THAT A TURKEY LEG DOESN'T GO IN A TRIFLE. LEARN TO KNOW WHEN A FOOD IDEA IS SHITE AND MOVE ON FROM IT OR JUST GET IN THE FUCKING SEA.

Fortnum's Ploughman's Pie

Another example of the wretched artisanalization of our standard food staples. Take something that costs next to nothing in a little shop down the precinct, fuck about with it negligibly and bung it out for ten times the price after putting the word 'artisanal' in its description.

(In case you're wondering, 'artisanal' means 'fucked up by arseholes'.)

If you're anything like me, you're probably not a regular customer in Fortnum & Mason, so there's little chance of you coming across their £30 ploughman's pie, but it's important that you know of its existence, in case you need a reason to boycott them.

Fortnum's later took this crusty monstrosity, available

on their website in the summer of 2015, off sale, probably following vigorous protests from pie rights campaigners. It can be had as part of their £115 Richmond Picnic selection, though, if you're that way inclined.

Thirty quid for a fucking pie. Thirty fucking quid. In a country where one of the major growth industries is the food bank. Fuck it all to death. Not the pie – the pie is probably really tasty.

GET YOUR SHITTY TOFF PIE IN THE FUCK-ING SEA AND STICK TO WHAT YOU'RE BEST AT – EATING SWANS AND BADGER BAITING.

Molecular gastronomy

According to Wikipedia, molecular gastronomy is 'a sub-discipline of food science that seeks to investigate the physical and chemical transformations of ingredients that occur in cooking. Its programme includes three axes, as cooking is recognized to have three components, which are social, artistic and technical.

'Molecular cuisine is a modern style of cooking, and takes advantage of many technical innovations from the scientific disciplines.'

In short, then, it's a load of old wank made up by bell ends in an attempt to prise cash out of the palms of the weary, the impressionable and the vulnerable.

IN THE FUCKING SEA YOU GO, FOOD
CHARLATANS.

Wine o'clock

You see it all over Twitter and Facebook, mostly on a
Friday but in truth it could be any day with a 'day' in it.
'Is it wine o'clock yet?' Meaning: 'Is it time for me to
abandon all of my work and/or parenting responsibil-
ities and lose myself in a haze of alcohol?'

Ha ha ha – but it's all good fun, isn't it? Lovely that
you're able to attach a twee catchphrase to functioning
alcoholism while your deadlines slip, your work targets
fly out of the window, and your kid sits on the kitchen
floor and bites into an Ariel liquitab.

STOP FUCKING ABOUT, GET YOURSELF
IN THE FUCKING SEA AND MAKE WINE
O'CLOCK 9.15 A. M. – YOU KNOW YOU
FUCKING WANT TO.

Hair in our white bread

You probably weren't expecting this piece of news but
yeah, there might well be human hair in your sliced loaf.
Sorry to be the bearer of this bad news, but there it is.
That's properly changed your life hasn't it?

L-Cysteine, an amino acid used to prolong shelf-life

in products such as commercial bread, can be found in duck and chicken feathers and cow horns, but most that's used in food is made from human hair.

If it's any consolation, there's only a *little* bit of it in there.

PUT ALL OF THE L-CYSTEINE IN THE FUCKING SEA.

Heritage tomatoes

Are you sitting comfortably? Good – here comes a short lecture on heritage tomatoes, or 'heirloom tomatoes'. Did you know there are four kinds? Yes, yes there are. You can choose from family heirlooms, commercial heirlooms, mystery heirlooms and created heirlooms.

The heirloom tomato is non-hybrid and open-pollinated, and some people say they taste better, although people usually say that sort of thing when they're trying to flog you something that costs a bit more than the normal price (see everything in the world that is organic).

Heritage tomatoes there, then. There's actually people walking among us who give a shit about this kind of thing.

TAKE YOUR FUCKING NAZI TOMATOES AND CHUCK THEM IN THE FUCKING SEA.

No, your eyes are not deceiving you, and your hands and mouths aren't getting bigger – the chocolate bars we lovingly cherish are gradually shrinking. Most of the big names have been giving us less and less of what we crave: our dark master, the cocoa bean.

It's part of a thing which so-called experts are calling 'shrinkflation' and which I am calling 'shitey chocolate manufacturers giving us less and charging us the same or even more'.

In 2013, it was reported that Mars bars had shrunk from 58g to 51g and Snickers bars from 58g to 48g, while their prices stayed the same. Meanwhile, Nestlé's Yorkie bar shrunk from 65g to 55g, losing an entire chunk. When it launched in 1976, a Yorkie was a whopping 70g.

Chocolate bars are just the thin end of the wedge, though, and shrinkflation is happening in products right across the board. The manufacturers want to find a price that we're happy to pay, and when production costs increase, their preferred alternative to hiking up that 'comfort price' is to just give us a little bit less than before and hope that we don't notice.

IF YOU WON'T GIVE US BACK OUR PROPER-SIZED CHOCOLATE BARS YOU NEED TO GET IN THE FUCKING SEA, YOU FACE-LESS CREW OF THIEVING ANTI-WONKAS. THEY'RE OUR HERITAGE AND OUR

BIRTHRIGHT AND OUR GATEWAY TO
LATER-LIFE DIABETES.

Christmas drinkers

Tis the season to be jolly, apparently, but if you're a
regular boozer it's the season to have your piss boiled as
the pubs are invaded by once-a-year fuckwits out with
their pals or workmates, ruining things for everyone
else.

Unused to drinking properly, he starts off in early
afternoon with everyone else, but is fucking hammered
by 3.30 p.m., stumbling into tables and kicking off with
the bar staff because he thinks they're ignoring him as
he waves his fiver in the air.

You'll also see him getting himself into overly familiar
conversations with nearby groups of women, crying
after a phone call with his wife goes wrong and then
throwing up in the street, uncomfortably close to where
the smokers stand.

He's as good an argument for the complete abolition
of Christmas as you're ever likely to come across and his
only saving grace is that he's only spotted once every
twelve months.

KNOW YOUR FUCKING PLACE, ARSE-
HOLE. THE ONLY STUFF YOU SHOULD BE
DRINKING AT THIS KEY POINT IN THE
CALENDAR IS THE FUCKING SEA WATER.

Krispy Kreme drive thrus

There can be no doubting that we've tipped over into the realms of total piggery when we can't even be arsed to use our fucking legs in order to get our hands on a box of high-end doughnuts, delicious as they truly are. Mmmm, glazed . . . mmmm, custard . . . mmmm, chocolate . . . mmmm, peanut butter . . .

Anyway . . . the various mouth-watering flavours aren't really the issue here (oh God, Lotus Caramelized Biscoff) – the point is that now that we've got Krispy Kreme drive thrus cropping up hither and thither, you can get your doughnut fix on wheels, eradicating even the slightest calorie expenditure before you get to cram them into your mouth with the joyless monotony of pushing a council tax reminder into a shredder.

Is it just cars, vans and motorcycles that can pass through the drive thru, though? What about those motorized wheelchairs? The oversized ones for those of us who are too obese to take more than a few steps without leaning against a wall, gasping for air and mopping our fevered brows with a flannel. We deserve our effort-free doughnuts too, surely?

LOOK AT US, KRISPY KREME. LOOK AT WHAT YOU'VE FUCKING WELL REDUCED US TO. DRIFTERS, SCOURING THE STREETS ON WHEELS, CRYING OUT FOR A DOUGH-NUT FIX BUT UNWILLING TO USE OUR

LEGS TO GET ONE. GET IN THE FUCK-
ING SEA.

The Dausage

There's a special place in the depths of the ocean reserved
just for the man (it's almost always a man) who decided
that a pork sausage injected with raspberry jam would
be something that the wider public might go ga-ga for.

But that's exactly what he did, combining a doughnut
with a sausage and creating what he opted to call the
'dausage'. The absolute fucker.

It's the kind of desperate idea that can only come to
life on the Kickstarter crowdfunding website, and that's
exactly where you'll find it. 'We are currently only able to
serve Dausages at food fayres and festivals, as we do not
have a machine capable of preparing Dausages,' bleats
its creator's Kickstarter page, leading you to imagine
him individually pumping jam into a string of cooked
sausages with his special jam syringe. It's a criminal psychologist's dream.

The dausage man has big plans, though – he's got an
entire range of warped meat products in mind. The 'recipe
ideas' section on his Kickstarter page cites such
future atrocities as pork and beef with custard, chicken
with raspberry jam, venison with strawberry custard,
dorizo, Cumberland dausage ring, dalami, dipolatas,
dankfurters and black dudding.

Duck off, you ducking dunt.

STICK YOUR FUCKING DAUSAGE UP YOUR
FUCKING ARSE, MATE – THEN GET IN
THE FUCKING SEA WITH IT.

Cucumber

Ninety-six per cent water and almost completely tasteless,
cucumber is somehow in vogue at the moment, which is
on a par with shunning chocolate bars for rice paper.

Some deluded arsehole even recently suggested using
a cucumber instead of two pieces of bread when making
a sandwich. Yes, just slice a cucumber down the middle
and then add ham, cheese and whatever else you need to
mask the fact that most of your lunch is a bland,
water-filled length of nothingness.

Have these fuckers got shares in cucumber farms? Is
there something being put in our cucumbers by the illu-
minati, designed to keep us docile? What other reasoning
could there be for this lame vegetable fuckery?

MAKE THEM 96 PER CENT SEA WATER
AND THEN AT LEAST THEY'D HAVE
SOME FUCKING FLAVOUR.

Insane supermarket recipe suggestions

'Mix it up this morning and add some spinach to your
beans on toast for a tasty treat,' tweeted Tesco recently.

No – fuck off – that shit is *not* acceptable. You've lazily made that up in the absence of having anything else of worth to say and you're just trying to get people's attention.

But hang on – perhaps there's something deeper going on here. The Tesco tweet came in the wake of a campaign of insane recipe suggestions from Sainsbury's, the absolute shit pinnacle of which was their notion that Bolognese sauce could be enhanced with a spoon or two of their instant coffee.

What's really going on here? Are representatives from the big supermarkets getting together in secret and brainstorming new ways in which they can slyly take the piss out of us? Can we expect to see Asda chirping up soon, urging us to beef up our breakfast cereals by adding a pinch of Bisto to the milk?

JUST SELL US SOME GROCERIES INSTEAD OF FUCKING WITH OUR HEADS WITH THESE PSYCHEDELIC SERVING SUGGESTIONS. TRY THE TASTE OF SEA WATER WITH FUCKING EVERYTHING, YOU ARSEHOLES.

Nando's

Looking for something a bit classier than Burger King but are inexplicably terrified of proper restaurants and tricky concepts like waiter service? Get yourself along to

Nando's, you lazy fucker, and check out the vibe that used to exist before all the youth clubs got shut down.

There's more types of chicken dishes than you can shake a wishbone at, with a wide variety of sides like corn on the cob and, erm . . . double chips. What's more, you can take in the sights and sounds of a load of under-twenty-fives titting about on their phones while you 'enjoy' your chicken. Happy with that? Really?

YOU CAN'T BE A RESTAURANT IF I HAVE TO GO UP TO THE COUNTER TO GET MYSELF ANOTHER DRINK. FUCK OFF INTO THE SEA.

Tea pubs

Let's face it, pubs were well and truly done for the moment they started serving food and letting kids in. It was a slippery slope after that, and once the smoking ban came into play and we all realized that the second most dominant smell in our boozers was the fucking drains, the demise of the pub as the community centre-piece was inevitable.

But now look what's happened: tea pubs. Like real pubs, but selling tea instead. More than 300 people collectively invested over £200,000 in some place called Brew (in London, obviously). The brainiac behind this scandalous concept, Alex Holland, said: 'Brew is a place with the atmosphere of a pub but instead of offering pints of beer, serving pots of tea. As well as serving loose-leaf throughout the day, at night it will provide tea cocktails like our Earl Grey and Tonic or Lapsang Old Fashioned.'

There's no hope for any of us. None whatsoever.

STOP CALLING IT A PUB. IT'S NOT A PUB, IT'S A FUCKING TEA ROOM. STOP TRYING TO FUCK UP PUBS. THEY'RE ALREADY FUCKED. FUCK OFF INTO THE SEA WITH YOUR FUCKING TEA ROOM, YOU FUCK-ING CLOWN.

Idiotic plate replacements

When we go into a pub or restaurant for some grub, we don't want it dished up on a fucking chopping board, shovel, roof tile or in a fucking bucket, as per the current trend.

We don't want our dinner handed to us in a fishing net, on a piece of laminate flooring, inside a pair of tights that have been stapled to an old Sinclair ZX Spectrum or hidden in an unnamed location that is only reachable with the help of a treasure map that has been drawn on a piece of parchment with a quill pen.

We don't want our fish and chips presented on top of a tiny replica piano, stuffed inside a top hat or secreted away inside a doll's house.

Fuck all that. Fuck it all to death.

JUST GIVE US OUR DINNER ON A FUCK-
ING PLATE OR GET IN THE FUCKING
SEA.

Wanky crisp flavours

Not crisps that specifically taste of wank (although
someone in Shoreditch will almost certainly be having a
lightbulb moment when they read those words), but
rather the inexcusable current trend for fucking about
with crisp flavours and trying to make them appear to
be more than what they are, which is . . . just a bag of
fucking crisps.

Among the needless rogue flavours that have crept
on to the shelves in the past few months are:

Free-range chicken, mustard and Worcester sauce: no one,
fucking *no one* has ever knocked back the offer of a packet
of chicken-flavoured crisps because they thought the
chicken in them might have been cage-reared, so get
over yourselves. Anyway, I checked, and Walkers' standard chicken crisps are free-range, but they don't bang on
about it. Fuck off.

Grouse and whinberry: What in the name of fuck is a
whinberry? I wouldn't recognize one if it crept in and
pissed in my eyeball while I slept. Behave.

Firecracker lobster: A firework-cooked lobster? What?
What?

Parmesan, asparagus and mustard: Better than cheese
and onion? Highly unlikely. Next!

164

Gin and tonic: Because G&T and fried potato snacks have always been a winning combination, yes? No.

Winter berries and prosecco with fizz and sparkle: This is just some cunt mucking about for a bet. Fuck it off.

Look, there should only be three flavours of crisps – plain, salt & vinegar and beef. That's it – anything else is frippery.

STOP FUCKING ABOUT WITH OUR CRISPS AND GET IN THE FUCKING SEA.

The French bar selling wine in baby bottles

There's a bar in France selling wine to adult customers in baby bottles with teats on them. That is all.

GET IN THE FUCKING SEA.

Juicing crawls

The cult of juicing in itself is bad enough – hordes of messed-up, broken individuals convincing themselves that everything will be better if only they can swallow down blended piles of cabbage, kale, beetroot, sprouts, damsons and fucking kumquats.

Worse still, some of these crazed self-abusers are ganging up and taking it to the streets, going on juicing crawls around London (fucking obviously), hitting the juice bars en masse and getting giddy on vomitous concoctions that smell like the kind of stuff you'd usually pour down your bog in an attempt to unblock the u-bend.

Just when you thought there could be nothing worse than a pub crawl that you're not part of, along comes the juice crawl, and now all bets are off.

GET IN THE FUCKING SEA. THE JUICY, JUICY SEA. IT TASTES A FUCKLOAD BETTER THAN KALE, THAT'S FOR CERTAIN.

Granola dust

It's a 'super food' apparently, which is always a surefire signifier that the taste of it will make you want to hurl your guts up. It'd be nice if it came ready-made in a box, even if it was from some creepy independent health food retailer, but no – you have to knock this shit together yourself.

You'll need oats, nuts and seeds, mixed and toasted in the oven for about twenty minutes before you add dried fruit, cocoa powder, ground coffee and orange zest. Only then does the dustification happen, in a food processor.

Once you've done all that, you can pour some into a bowl and enjoy your delicious dusty breakfast. Alternatively, you could just stir a tablespoon of strawberry jam into a bowl of play sand and eat that instead; you'll probably get the same feeling from it.

The pioneer of this atrocity? Why that'd be Jamie fucking Oliver. Obviously.

MIX THIS SHIT WITH A MILLION GAL-
LONS OF SEA WATER AND THEN FORGET
ABOUT THE FUCKER FOR EVER.

Wine tasting

Complete and utter shit and nonsense, by and for people
who (a) don't know how to have fun properly; (b) har-
bour dark UKIP feelings but know better than to air
them publicly.

The entire wine-tasting industry is an elaborate lie –
the Emperor's New Clothes of booze, with everyone
involved maintaining the pretence out of fear that they'll
look stupid if they question it all for even a few
seconds.

Just have some wine and enjoy yourself. Drink a couple of bottles if you can manage it, *without* gobbing any
of it out into a jug. Don't try and identify flavours and
aromas that aren't even fucking there – talk instead
about films and music you love, places you've been and
the brilliant people you've known.

Wine tasting – nein danke.

TRY TASTING THE SUBTLE BLEND OF
SALT AND MORE FUCKING SALT THAT IS
INHERENT IN A GALLON OF RANCID
SEA WATER INSTEAD.

Hipster Shit

Silicon Roundabout

Splonked right in the middle of that deplorable peak hipster area of Old Street/Shoreditch, the 'cultural commentators' reckon this place is some kind of creative hub where some of London's brightest and best tech talents assemble and work their magic, coming up with brilliant new . . . well, apps and websites.

Because we're really short on apps and websites, aren't we? There's a veritable fucking gulf of them. And like everything else, the 97 per cent rule applies – namely that 97 per cent of them are total shit.

The truth is that Silicon Roundabout seems to be nothing more than a playpen for blokes called Barnaby to hang around in, playing oversized versions of Ker-Plunk and Buckaroo, stopping only to lounge around on beanbags and brainstorm a bit about their new app, which is designed to tell you the location of your nearest family-planning-clinic-themed bar.

WE NEED TO GET A FLEET OF HELICOPTERS TO WINCH THIS 'ROUNDABOUT' OF FUCKNUTS UP INTO THE AIR AND THEN CAREFULLY TRANSPORT IT THIRTY

MILES EAST OF MARGATE BEFORE
PLUNGING IT INTO THE FUCKING SEA.
AND THEN MERCILESSLY BOMBING THE
SHIT OUT OF IT.

Hackney Colliery Band

For decades, the inhabitants of mining towns and villages used culture as a way of binding their communities and providing an escape from the horrific working conditions that they had to endure in order to put food on the table for their loved ones.

Coal mining was a truly diabolical way of earning a living – the men who ventured underground each day did so not knowing if they would make it out alive again at the end of their shift.

Their brass bands provided a release valve that they could be proud of – an expression of their solidarity and aspiration for a better existence.

As far as I am aware, East London has no coal-mining history whatsoever. Sure, there's a 'Hackney Shaft' in the Twickenham Platinum Mine, but that's in fucking South Africa.

But the absence of any kind of colliery activity hasn't stopped the progress of the Hackney Colliery Band, a gang of parping arriviste hipsters who have shamelessly hijacked the concept.

Their website speaks of 'mining nuggets of funk, hip-hop and high-octane rock from the musical coalface and throwing in a few chunks of Balkan brass, ska and contemporary jazz for good measure'.

Ahhhhh . . . so they're *musical* miners, as opposed to coal miners! They should come up with a different name, then – like the Hackney Wankers Band.

STOP STEALING WORKING-CLASS CUL-TURE AND PASSING IT OFF AS YOUR OWN, YOU FUCKING DISGUSTING HIPSTER PRICKS. GET BACK TO YOUR CEREAL SCULPTURES AND YOUR CLOCKWORK STROGANOFF OR GET IN THE FUCK-ING SEA.

A bloke who wore a Ghostbusters suit for a week

Here's a quirky little tale – for reasons best known to himself and his editor, CNET 'journalist' Danny Gallagher donned a Ghostbusters suit that he'd made himself and wandered around his Dallas neighbourhood for a week, just to see how people would react.

Ahead of the new, female-skewed reimagining of the film franchise, Danny said: 'Someone has to bring those uniforms back, and fast, before the new uniforms completely replace their memory.' He's talking utter shit, obviously – you could comfortably fit everyone in the world who gives a shit about the heritage of the Ghost-busters uniforms into a Nissan Micra.

But just how would folk react to Danny as he took to the streets dressed up like a 1980s movie comedy character? Would he face open mockery, sympathetic pats on the back, or would he be inundated with requests of help with spook destruction from random strangers?

After all, the good people at CNET had gone to the trouble of commissioning an entire online article about his 'social experiment', so you'd expect the results to be enlightening.

No. A few people stared at Danny, and that was about it. Which is pretty much as you'd expect when he's going around Dallas dressed as Dan Aykroyd's awkward cousin.

'I Wore a Ghostbusters Suit for a Week and Some People Stared a Bit' should have been the title *and* the entire body of copy. Or 'I Am a Fucking Twat'.

NEVER MIND BEING STARED AT, YOU FUCKING GOON – YOU'RE LUCKY YOU WEREN'T SCOOPED UP BY A BIG NET OR TRANQUILLIZED BY DALLAS MENTAL HEALTH OFFICIALS. IF THERE WAS ANY JUSTICE THEY'D HAVE DRIVEN YOU TO THE COAST IN THE BACK OF A MASSIVE VAN AND DEPOSITED YOU IN THE FUCK-ING SEA. WHO YA GONNA CALL NOW, FUCKO?

The Beard Bib

In decades to come, having eventually recovered from the inevitable psychological trauma that will follow the inevitable Great Shave and the revelation that some of our menfolk have ordinary-shaped, bald chins, our children will ask: 'What the titting fuck was that beard thing all about? Why did everyone want to look like a Victorian cricketer?'

Trust me – the hipster beard craze will eventually pass, to be replaced by LED contact lenses or something, but the horror of the accessories will live long in the memory.

For example, once things return to normal, the inventors of the Beard Bib will be shunned by polite society, and rightly so. Sold via the Beard King website (which is almost certainly run by a cunt as opposed to a king) for just £20, the bib fastens around the neck and can be attached to a supporting wall, creating a facial hammock designed to catch clippings when you're trimming and sculpting your beard, just before you head off out to look like a desperate trend-following fucking arsehole down the pub with all your other imagination-free, beard-sporting twat pals.

Fuck off and die, Beard Bib.

PERHAPS A BETTER ALTERNATIVE WOULD BE A BIB THAT TIGHTLY SURROUNDS THE ENTIRE FACE, CAUSING

ASPHYXIATION AND AN ALARMINGLY
QUICK AND PAINFUL BEARD-RELATED
DEATH. FOLLOWED BY BURIAL IN THE
FUCKING SEA.

Vinegar-drinking classes

We've all done it – forced by reduced financial circumstances into opting for a disgustingly cheap bottle of
wine. Maybe something from Estonia or Uzbekistan.
You know there's only a 3 per cent chance that it'll be
half decent but you take the risk anyway.

Big mistake – you open it, pour out a glass, take a sip and
gob it down the sink. 'Fuck off – tastes like vinegar,' you
bark, your evening ruined. You're right – why would anyone want to drink vinegar? They do, though. The twats.

The Raw Duck restaurant in . . . wait for it . . . Hackney recently put on some vinegar-drinking classes,
presumably for anyone with more spare time than sense
and a weird loathing of their own taste buds.

Participants got to sample a 'small, seasonal selection
of drinking vinegars' and could even learn how to make
their own at home. And it'd only cost you £15 for the
privilege! There's an incredibly short leap from drinking
vinegar to eating salt out of a cereal bowl. Keep watching – it'll happen.

YOU KNOW WHAT ELSE TASTES OF SALT,
DON'T YOU? THE FUCKING SEA – SO IN

173

YOU GO WITH YOUR VINEGAR-DRINKING BULLSHIT.

School dinners pop-up restaurant

Ahhh, school. Best days of your life, etc., etc. Unless you were lucky enough to have your education paid for, there was the run-down infrastructure, the peer pressure, the bullying, the bouncing hormones, all of the workload and very little disposable income. Better than adulthood? Fuck that.

Then there were the school dinners. Signature dishes included coloured slop with rice, grey slop with overdone potatoes, fishcakes doused in blood, curry that could easily have put you off curry for life.

As for desserts, take your pick from dry, flavourless cake that was forced into a splodge of custard thick enough to stand a pencil up in it. Or . . . no, that was about it.

Serve it all on long tables with kids sat in rows and trying to avoid being slapped on the back of the head for making a noise or not eating quickly enough and you've got an experience that would make a long weekend among the starving of Ethiopia seem like a decent break.

It's not the sort of thing you would want to replicate . . . unless you were the sort of absolute fucker who is looking to make a quick buck from a pop-up experience dining experience fiasco experience.

Well, look at what we have here! It's After School

Club, a pop-up fuckery food hole, serving fish fingers and alphabetti spaghetti to morons in London in the summer of 2015.

Not only would you get that, you were also promised theatre, music, homework and milk monitors, in what seemed to be a lovely way to get away from the horrors of your adult life – if you were inclined to dig deep into your piggy bank and pay *fifty-five pounds* of your hard-earned 'pocket money'.

THE CUNTS RESPONSIBLE FOR THIS SHOULD HAVE THEIR HEADS FLUSHED DOWN THE SCHOOL TOILETS, AS VITAL PREPARATION FOR THEIR VISIT TO THE FUCKING SEA.

Beard beer

Like beer? Like beards? This should be a boozy flavour heaven for you then – a bottled beer that has been crafted using the yeast from the facial fuzz of brewmaster John Maier.

No, really – follicles from Maier's beard (which he's been growing since 1978) have turned out to contain yeast that is perfect for brewing beer, which is almost a full house if you're playing Hipster Bingo.

To the casual observer, it might seem like a semi-legal abomination, causing you to reach for your environmental health guidebooks. We can only pray that Maier was extracting this 'beard yeast' with an independent witness in the room and that he wasn't getting it from 'somewhere else'.

According to its website, the beer is best served with beef, dessert, poultry and pork and it also states that there are 'no chemicals, additives, or preservatives'. That's admirable, but . . .

THERE'S A CLANGING CHIME OF DOOM RINGING THROUGH MY HEAD HERE – THE FUCKING BEARD YEAST. GET IT IN THE FUCKING SEA.

Come Fry With Me *restaurant*

Chips are up there with ice cream and masturbation in the short, short list of things everyone in the world loves, so it makes perfect sense that someone should open a restaurant devoted to the delicious sticklets of deep-fried potato. After all, we've already got ice cream parlours and a wanking-based food experience is something that belongs in niche movies.

But do you feel as though a specialist chip restaurant isn't enticing enough? I agree, and so did Tiffany Plant who also gave her central London restaurant an additional . . . aviation theme. No, really. Because chips and aviation go together hand in hand, like Morris dancing and milkshakes, right?

Apparently the inspiration for the deranged project

came when Tiffany experienced truffle-Parmesan fries: a side dish so delicious she couldn't understand why it could not take 'centre stage'.

The clue here is 'side dish'. It's why we don't have restaurants that only sell onion rings or crisps.

As for the flying theme, fuck only knows what that's about. There's also a Fry Truck – a van that will allow you to try this piece of shit idea at an outdoor location.

Fry Truck. Truck like a plane. No, it's just total bollocks.

TRUCK OFF AND FRY AND GET IN THE FUCKING SEA.

Ball pool meeting rooms

With its suits, coffee, flipcharts and furrowed brows, the business meeting is an arena that is in desperate need of being lightened up, or 'funkified', or 'fucked up for no good reason'.

But business meetings don't have to be so po-faced, do they? Surely they can be *fun* too, right? Wrong. If you're someone who has allowed themselves to be immersed in that world, you deserve everything you fucking well get. Fun is not on the menu for you – if you can fit a bit of fun in after you clock off from your turgid careerism at 9 p.m. each night then good for you. Otherwise, leave the fun to the loafers and the shirkers.

The pursuit of good vibes and endorphins while at the same time landing contracts, clinching deals and blue-sky strategificating has resulted in the funky horror show that is the ball pool meeting room – where adult infantilization meets the serious world of hard commerce, and a worrying growing trend.

Fuck knows what you're supposed to do if you're called into a meeting in a ball pool room and you're one of those people who take their job seriously. Do you sit at the side and try to maintain some decorum while all the other twats bounce about in their rainbow-coloured nitwit pit? Or join in half-heartedly, tossing the occasional ball in the air and mournfully saying, 'Whoop. Look, we really need to discuss the problems in the Stockport office now . . . '

TRY HAVING YOUR BUSINESS MEETINGS IN THE FUCKING SEA – YOUR DEFINITION OF FUN WILL SOON CHANGE.

Cassette Store Day

As times change, so too does technology, and the way we consume music has been getting easier and easier with each generation. But vinyl has stubbornly hung on in there, and even has its own special Record Store Day, where idiots get to shell out for overpriced limited editions of music that's mostly already available on other formats.

Fair play to vinyl and Record Store Day, though – it's done well to stick around. The more recent and considerably worse Cassette Store Day, though? That can go fuck itself right in the eye. Anyone who is playing music on cassette in 2015 is either a showy, look-at-me prick or someone who has 10,000 cassettes stored in neatly piled storage boxes in their bedroom and can't stop because it makes them feel safe.

Oh, and no one ever said, 'I'm just off down the cassette store.' It isn't, wasn't and never will be a thing.

AND ANYWAY, IT'S 'TAPES' NOT 'CASSETTES', YOU FUCKING KNOBHEADS. GET IN THE FUCKING SEA WITH YOUR C-90S.

Gentlemen's Afternoon Tea

'Where are you off to then, Brian?'

'Gnnmmnens aaanon te.'

'You what?'

'Gentlemen's . . . Afternoon Tea.'

'You're taking the piss, right?'

'Erm . . . '

'What's it all about then? What do you get?'

'Well, there's traditional English savouries such as wild boar sausage rolls, miniature steak and ale pies and warm, wookey hole cheddar and bacon scones – accompanied by single malt scotch.'

'Fuck me, mate. How much are they charging you for that?'

'£34.50.'

'And is it *really* going to be any better than a couple of cans of Stella and a pork pie while you watch Channel 4 Racing?'

'Erm . . .'

'Brian, you're a fucking prick.'

LOOK, WE'RE ALL STRUGGLING JUST TO STAY ALIVE HERE. AFFORDABLE FOOD IS SCARCE TO COME BY, AND SOME OF US HAVE BEEN REDUCED TO NIB-BLING ON THE WALLPAPER IN ORDER TO SURVIVE UNTIL GIRO DAY. PIMPING OVERPRICED NIBBLES TO BEARD WAX-SNIFFERS IS JUST RUBBING SALT INTO SOCIETY'S GAPING WOUND AND IT NEEDS TO BE CATAPULTED RIGHT INTO THE FUCKING SEA.

Coppers wearing beard nets

The police are no different to the rest of us, there to pro-tect and serve . . . or something, but we're increasingly all in it together . . . and that. As such, it seems that they're just as prone to the whims of modern life as we all are. That's a fairly waffly, roundabout way of saying: *fucking hell – we've got hipster cops now.*

It all started when photos of that riot officer emerged; you know, the one with the oiled moustache of a circus strongman, coupled with the beard of a Victorian cricketer. He looked less inclined to break up a mass civil disturbance and more likely to be found in a gin palace, wearing loafers with no socks and perusing a magazine article about how shaved tripe is the new pulled pork.

His appearance sent the internet crazy with memes, 95 per cent of which were woeful, obviously, but alarm bells obviously started ringing at the HQ of the Gloucestershire Constabulary. It wasn't long before revised uniform guidelines were introduced, which included . . . beard nets.

Perfect for reinforcing the image of police officers as no-nonsense upholders of law and order? Or a surefire way of making them look as though they're working in a pre-packed sandwich factory on the outskirts of Budapest?

Bearded cops, you have a choice – either shave it off or face the ridicule of every single member of the public from age two to 222.

THERE'S PLENTY OF NETS FOR YOU IN THE FUCKING SEA, YOU SICK BASTARDS.

Public typewriter users

We're all busy people these days, and some of us need to work on the move, taking advantage of free public wi-fi, allowing us to whip out our laptops, tablets and phones so that we can 'touch base' and 'have another crack at level 53 of Candy Crush'.

What if you don't have an electronic device? Simple – just travel around with your typewriter under your arm and use that in public instead. Yes, believe it or not, there have been sightings of people (well, hipsters to be more precise) brandishing typewriters in coffee shops, parks and other places where they can expect to be seen by passers-by. Seen, photographed and exposed on social media.

Typewriters. Big, fuck-off bulky ones, like Ernest Hemingway would have used in the olden days. Lazy work really – any true hipster would be adopting a sleeker, more portable and more nerdish typewriter, as last used in about 1982. But we're here to denigrate these arseholes, not advise them.

These thick-headed attention-seekers need to either take it to another level – namely sitting in the middle of Starbucks and writing in a massive, dusty ledger with a quill – or fuck off altogether. Preferably to a cave, where they can paint on the fucking walls.

IF YOU WANT US ALL TO LOOK AT YOU, DO SOMETHING WORTHWHILE INSTEAD OF POSING IN A PARK WITH A FUCKING SMITH CORONA. WEAR A REVOLV- ING BOW TIE THAT LIGHTS UP. AMUSE RATHER THAN ENRAGE. OR JUST GET IN THE FUCKING SEA.

Man Buns

Men's heads have been getting it in the neck over the past couple of years. Once the tedious beard craze had got a grip of popular culture, the trendsetters didn't look far for their next project, but like pop groups and that 'difficult second album', there was a reek of desperation about the 'man bun'.

Yes, the fucking man bun – long-haired men were given the go ahead to tie their locks up atop their bonce as if it was the most natural thing in the world. This deranged fad even had its own poster boy – a preening fuck-knuckle who goes by the name of Brock O'Hurn.

A star of Instagram (because *there's* a status symbol you'd be a fool not to crave), Brock posts endless snaps of him looking moody with his mane all bundled up on the top of his head. Imagine an airbrushed Brad Pitt that has had his brains knocked out with a shovel and that's pretty much Brock for you.

Coming soon – men with wheels of hair on the sides of their head like Princess Leia. Doom.

THE ONLY IMPROVEMENT TO YOUR HEAD THAT I CAN THINK OF WOULD BE TO SEE IT BEING BOOTED INTO THE FUCKING SEA BY A GIANT.

Man braids

Has the man bun been and gone already? Fuck me, that was quick – I didn't even get the chance to grow my hair long enough to put it in a bun. Bit of a heads-up would be nice next time, eh?

Just weeks after we thought the man bun had taken us to a level of peak cuntiness, the impatient, self-appointed shitweasels who seem to dictate hair trends were bigging up the braid, telling men that it was okay to go around looking like a loaf of artisan bread, even if it meant attracting the derision of all and sundry while they went about it.

God help us if there's a war – we'd be well and truly fucked with these hair-sculpting knuckleheads pitching in.

GET IN THE FUCKING SEA AND LET YOUR LOCKS FLOW WILD AND FREE – MAYBE WITH THEM GETTING SNAGGED ON A JAGGED ROCK AND BEING RIPPED FROM YOUR SCALP. TWATS.

Crocheted man shorts

At a secret location, probably underground and probably in Dalston (fucking obviously) the hipster elders gathered together and held an important meeting.

'We've had an exciting new proposal, which we think will enhance our image and enrage the public at large into the process.'

'Tell us of it, Senior Hipster.'

'Shorts. For men.'

'Good – worn ironically, in winter?'

'They can be – that's because they are crocheted.'

'Oh, that's wonderful.'

'Available in many, many bright colours. So lurid that they'll take the heat away from the lumberjack beards completely.'

'This is a magnificent development. I'll alert my contacts at *Dazed & Confused* magazine, and they should be able to have pictures of the shorts on their website by early afternoon.'

'Marvellous. We're never going to stop, are we?'

'No. We are the hipsters. We cannot be stopped.'

CROCHETED FUCKING MAN SHORTS. HIGH WATER-RETENTION PROPERTIES, MEANING THAT ESCAPE FROM THE FUCKING SEA WILL BE NIGH ON FUCKING IMPOSSIBLE.

The 'Cereal Killer' café

Public opinion swayed in favour of the pair of dicksplats responsible for this abominable waste of space, energy and time not too long ago when it was targeted by anti-gentrification protestors in Shoreditch. Their café was shouted at a bit and splattered with paint in what the cereal twins described as a 'hate crime'. This was a helpful statement as their total inability to recognize what a true hate crime is and their need to tag themselves as an oppressed minority instantly wiped away a vast amount of that aforementioned sympathy.

The only minority these pricks belong to is the one that thinks it's a great idea to flog bowls of Frosties to complete arseholes for three pound fifty a pop and try to justify it all by saying that some of your cereals are imported from the USA and that you've got fourteen different types of milk to choose from.

As if that legitimizes it. As if that makes taking the business model of a primary school breakfast club and trying to make your living from it in one of the most ludicrous and expensive cities on the planet a good thing somehow.

It's the thin end of the wedge and will only encourage and empower similar chancing shitehawks. Next thing you know we'll have mock sweet shops selling ten pence mix-ups for a fiver a bag, and artisan ice cream vans flogging 99s with a lump of Green & Black's hanging out of the top for a tenner.

THESE BEARDED TWATHOLES SHOULD BE PIMPING OUT RICE KRISPIES FROM THE OCEAN BED, AND IF YOU BUY INTO THIS SHIT, YOU'RE JUST AS MUCH A PART OF THE FUCKING PROBLEM SO YOU CAN GET IN THERE WITH THEM, YOU IDIOTS.

Earth's Fifty Worst Humans: Part 4

20 Jack Whitehall

Forty years ago, the 'king of comedy' was undoubtedly Tommy Cooper – a genius at delivery, timing and performing inept magic tricks so brilliantly that he made it look as though he didn't have a clue what he was doing. Cooper was a multi-faceted comedy dynamo and we'll probably never see his like again.

For three successive years from 2012, the lanky, posh, fucknugget Jack Whitehall was crowned King of Comedy at the British Comedy Awards, arguably bringing the words 'king' and 'comedy' into disrepute until the sun explodes and brings humanity's inglorious reign to a fiery, violent conclusion.

Crown Prince of Fist-Gnawingly Tedious Wankers, perhaps. King of Comedy? No. Perhaps fittingly, the British Comedy Awards did not take place in 2015, probably as a result of a deep sense of shame.

YOUR 'HUMOUR' WILL NOT BE APPRECIATED BY THE OCEAN'S WILDLIFE, WHITEHALL. IF THERE'S ANY JUSTICE THEY'LL HAVE YOUR FUCKING LEG OFF.

19 Benedict Cumberbatch

With a face like an anagram and voice that's even posher than those luxury biscuits that you'd never even *consider* buying, Cumberbatch (crazy name, annoying guy) hasn't done anything all that wrong but the fucker keeps cropping up everywhere. and there was that time when he had a major whinge about being discriminated against for being posh (mate, no, that's never a thing).

Oh, and there's *Sherlock*, and his 'mind palace'. Yes, that should suffice. Definitely one of the fifty worst people alive today.

GET IN THE FUCKING SEA, YOU POSH PRICK.

18 Boris Johnson

Can we just abandon that well-worn image of Johnson being some kind of shambling, bumbling shaft of light on the dark political scene? Gone? Good – because it's a load of old bollocks, and he's a cunning, conniving, hyper-ambitious cock of the highest order.

He's not dim, he's not confused and he's not charming either. He's a ruthless political beast with more salaried jobs than any human being can realistically do (MP, Mayor of London, journalist and soon-to-be biographer of Shakespeare, for which he's picking up a cool £500,000).

Oh, and stop calling him 'Boris' – you make him sound like the loveable buffoon he's pretending to be. Call him 'Johnson' or 'that twat'. Thanks.

YOU'RE FOOLING NO ONE, YOU POISON-OUS FUCKWAD – THE SEA IS THE BEST PLACE FOR YOU AND YOUR PRETENDY BURBLING AND MUMBLING.

17 Jarryd Zankovic

'I'm a funny hybrid between beauty therapist and tradie.' That's a sentence that came out of the mouth of the senior art director at Australia's Play Communications agency, and was just one of the phrases that earned him the title of Australia's Biggest Wanker in the press. He's bigger than that – this fucker is global.

Not convinced? In an interview with *B&T* Magazine, he went on to say: 'My style generally resembles simple colours and quality. It's sort of effortless.'

Jarryd hates the word 'hipster' but admits that he kind of fits the bill. 'You know . . . beard, no socks, drop crotch – which is really comfortable, especially for a dude who has a bit going on between his legs . . . ' he added before the world spewed up collectively.

Hipsters – and they wonder why they're so intensely disliked . . .

ON THE ONE HAND, IT'S GOOD THAT
WE'VE GOT SOMEONE TO FOCUS ON
WHO EPITOMIZES EVERYTHING THAT IS
LOATHSOME ABOUT THE MODERN HIP-
STER. ON THE OTHER HAND, HE NEEDS
TO JUST GET IN THE FUCKING SEA
IMMEDIATELY.

16 Mrs Mumford

Because of her fucking sons.

FUNDING MUST BE MADE FOR THE CRE-
ATION OF A TIME MACHINE SO THAT
MRS MUMFORD CAN GO BACK AND BE
PUT IN THE FUCKING SEA INSTEAD OF
PROCREATING AND UNLEASHING HER
CHILDREN'S CAMPAIGN OF 'AUTHENTIC'
MUSICAL SHITHOUSERY ON A PUBLIC
THAT IS TOO FUCKING MORONIC TO
REALIZE WHAT IT'S SIGNED UP FOR.

15 Chris Moyles

We thought we'd won. We thought he'd gone. Cut loose
from Radio 1 and seemingly a throwback to a darker,
less enlightened time, it felt as though we'd remember Moyles as the bloke who once commanded a

listenership of millions but ended up making his own vlogs on YouTube, where he painstakingly showed viewers how to make a fruit smoothie.

But then along came the geezer-heavy Radio X, a perfect stage for Moyles' wearisome, laddish shite and now the battle for all that is right and good has commenced yet again.

We must not forget his proposal to Charlotte Church, where he offered to: 'lead her through the forest of sexuality' after she had reached the age of sixteen. We must not forget the time when he referred to female listeners as 'dirty whores' for urinating in the shower.

We must not forget the time when he rejected a ringtone on air, describing it as 'gay'. We must not forget the thirty-minute, self-indulgent rant that time when Radio 1 hadn't paid him.

All of this must surely still be in him. We must not forget.

THE FACT THAT YOU HAVE BEEN GIVEN ANOTHER CHANCE TO POLLUTE THE EARS AND MINDS OF THE POPULATION IS ARGUABLY THE MOST SIGNIFICANT RADIO-RELATED CRIME SINCE JIMMY SAVILE FIRST BLEW A RING OF CIGAR SMOKE AT A MICROPHONE. THANKFULLY, YOUR BROADCASTING EQUIPMENT WILL NOT WORK EFFECTIVELY ONCE IT IS LYING ON THE OCEAN BED. GET IN THE FUCKING SEA, MOYLES.

14 Ricki Hall

Sporting the de rigueur tit-length beard, sculpted hair-style and pigshit-dim expression, model Ricki described his look in 2015 as: 'more gothic and bohemian, like vibrant Russell Brand with paisley'.

But that wasn't the worst of it. Quizzed on where he finds inspiration for such a look, Hall dropped the bomb. 'I take style tips from everything, even kids and homeless people. They can put anything together and it just works.'

Woah – wait. Homeless people? You're scouring the streets, seeking out vagrants in order to check out their threads so you can rip off their look? That's a fucking bold admission, Ricki but one that you'd expect from someone who looks so self-absorbed that he probably sleeps inside a mirrored box armed with half a dozen packets of wet wipes. You woeful fucking shitpipe.

DON'T PRETEND THAT BEING CHUCKED IN THE FUCKING SEA IS SOMETHING YOU ENJOY DOING IRONICALLY JUST SO YOU CAN SCORE A FEW EASY HIPSTER POINTS. YOU'RE GOING IN REGARDLESS.

13 Prince Philip

National treasure? Or pampered, cantankerous, racist, swan-eating bell end? It's the question that has occupied our minds for decades now, but fucking hell, there's only one answer, isn't there?

And your sons are a gang of arseholes as well, which speaks volumes about you.

HOW MANY MORE YEARS OF YOUR BEL-LIGERENT SHITHOUSERY DO WE HAVE TO ENDURE, YOU CROTCHETY OLD CUNT-PIECE? EMBRACE YOUR NAVAL HERITAGE AND GET IN THE FUCKING SEA.

12 *Dave Grohl*

Have you heard 'This Is A Call', the first single from Foo Fighters' debut album, released back in 1995? You have? Great – that's pretty much everything you need to hear from them, then. The rest is just Dave being a 'great guy' while churning out music for people whose brains can't quite understand music properly.

GET IN THE FUCKING SEA, YOU DREARY PURVEYOR OF WEAK MUSICAL PISS.

11 *Gregg Wallace*

Throughout the glory years of *Masterchef*, it hasn't been hard to suspect that Gregg Wallace is a complete span-ner. After all, he isn't even a chef – the cue-ball-headed irritant established himself as a greengrocer before lucking his way on to the telly.

But it's on Twitter where Gregg has consistently revealed himself to be a world-class prick. One of his recent tweets reeked of superiority, boasting: 'Meeting accountants & lawyers. May well stop at champagne bar at station on the way home.' Wow – important enough to have meetings with accountants and lawyers *and* doing well enough to be able to afford champagne too! Ooooh, can we all be like you, Gregg? Pleeeeease?

Arguably his finest moment on Twitter (matched only by the time someone tweeted a picture of himself giving Gregg the finger) came when a Tweeter called @valetudocage dropped the great man a line to see if he could help out with a charitable venture.

The conversation went like this:

@valetudocage: Hi Greg I am cycling just over 180 miles in
2 days for Macmillan Cancer Support. Any chance of a RT
(link to charity donation page)
@GreggAWallace: Gregg?
@valetudocage: No worries mate, it's only people with cancer. You worry about your extra G. Mastertwat.

Priceless. And from now on, whenever he appears on our screens, it is bad etiquette not to point and shout 'Mastertwat!' at your TV.

(G)GET IN THE FUCKING SEA, GREG(G).

Miscellaneous Fuckery

The Chilean miners

Thoroughly disappointed in the way these lads have conducted themselves. Back in 2010 they were the world's underground sweethearts – united in their race against time and a dwindling supply of oxygen.

Remember how we gasped as they were pulled out of the mine one by one? We gave them all pet names – Weepy Miner, Squinty Miner, Semi-Conscious Miner, Manic Miner, and we all fought over which one we liked best.

But just what have they done for us lately? Sure, there's a film starring Antonio Banderas, but the lads themselves have been more than a little quiet since their harrowing month-long ordeal.

Come on, fellas – give us something to cling to. Surely you must have written at least an album's worth of songs while you were down there. Maybe a few of you could buy a van and drive around solving mysteries like the Scooby Doo gang.

Don't tell us you're just trying to get on with your lives – you sought out your fame and you can't just switch it off again because it suits you.

WE OWN YOU, YOU FUCKERS. YOU TOOK OUR HEARTS AND YOU'RE GIVING US THE SQUARE ROOT OF FUCK ALL IN RETURN. GET IN THE FUCKING SEA, AND IF YOU FEEL LIKE IT, ORCHES-TRATE SOME KIND OF DRAMATIC SURVIVAL/RESCUE NARRATIVE.

'Special' days of the year

Every single fucking day, without fail — something is being celebrated or highlighted or marked in the calendar, and we're supposed to have some kind of response to it.

8 September? Salami Day, apparently. 6 July? Take Your Webmaster To Lunch Day. I wish I was making this up but I'm really not.

22 November? The start of International Chip Pan Fire Fortnight. Okay, so I'm making that one up. Fuck you, though — you thought it was real.

14 February? Valenti . . . no . . . it's Cream-Filled Chocolate Day, you fucking idiot. Didn't get laid on the 14th? Treat your dildo to something nice on the 18th instead, when it'll be Battery Day.

Who in the name of fuck gets to decide this shit and with whom do they register it all? Is there an official organization that logs these self-appointed days, or do they get chosen by an international committee? *Is Nigel*

Farage involved somehow? So many questions and no one around with any authority to answer them.

WE MUST REMAIN VIGILANT ABOUT THE INFERNAL SHIT AND FUCKERY THAT THREATENS TO SUFFOCATE US EVERYWHERE WE GO – THEREFORE EVERY SINGLE DAY NEEDS TO BE GET IN THE FUCKING SEA DAY.

David Cameron's mast

There must be a thousand reasons why David Cameron should be dwelling in the depths of the ocean for ever and ever amen, and that's being kind to the ham-faced lord of absolute fuckery.

You could fill a spin-off book on this one with all of the heinous plans and schemes that he has presided over throughout his tawdry life – the time when he left his kid in a pub is one of my favourites, not to mention the time when he forgot that he's supposed to be a lifelong supporter of Aston Villa and told a press conference that his team is West Ham.

That one was a couple of weeks before a general election – a time when you're supposed to look as honest and as genuine as you possibly can. And yet the cunt still won.

But if there's one story that speaks volumes about the

naked, self-serving shithousery of the man who repeatedly told us that we're all in it together, it's the announcement of the Cornwall mobile phone mast.

The mast, to be placed at Polzeath, was estimated to be costing £300,000 of the taxpayer's cash but would benefit the occupants of just seventy-four homes in the village.

Completely coincidentally, Polzeath is also Cameron's favourite holiday destination, and he has been previously heard to whinge about the absence of a decent mobile signal in the area, which is presumably stopping the fucker from making and taking calls about how he can fuck the poor and grind Britain further into the dirt while he enjoys building sandcastles and eating ice cream.

IT'S PROBABLY JUST A MASSIVE COINCIDENCE REALLY, BUT IT'D BE NICE TO SEE CAMERON STRAPPED TO THE TOP OF A MOBILE PHONE MAST ON THE POLZEATH BEACH BEFORE IT IS HACKED DOWN, WITH IT AND HIM FALLING INTO THE FUCKING SEA AS IT TOPPLES.

Prince Charles' new harpist

In July 2015, George Osborne stood before the House of Commons and delivered the first Budget under the new Conservative government. No longer hampered by the coalition with the Liberal Democrats, it was his first chance to properly flex his muscles and give the nation's poor the good, hard fucking they surely deserved.

Tax credits were chopped, benefit caps were reduced, and if you've got more than two children, you can basically forget about surviving on the breadline – you'll probably have to sell those surplus youngsters in order to pay for heating and supermarket-brand Weetabix.

If all of that wasn't wretched enough, a mere ninety minutes before Osborne unleashed his clanging chimes of doom, a missive was released from the court of the Prince of Wales. His royal highness had appointed a new official harpist!

Surely that would be all the consolation you would need on a day when you learned that the money you needed to survive was being grabbed away in order to help the nation recover from that economic crash that you had fuck all to do with in the first place.

Okay, so you found yourself looking at regular trips to the local food bank, augmented with snacks such as fried wallpaper and soup made from foraged dandelions, but look on the bright side – the heir to the throne has got himself fixed up with a new harpist! Can you imagine how good *he's* feeling today? Makes it all worthwhile . . .

GET IN THE SEA, YOU PAMPERED, JUG-EARED FUCKWAD, AND TAKE YOUR NEW PERSONAL STRING PLUCKER WITH YOU.

Sting makes two appearances in this book, which is nothing to be proud of whatsoever. This entry commemorates his horrific appearance on a yacht owned by the *Daily Mail* and moored at Cannes during the annual Lions festival.

It gets worse – also present and gurning as the Geordie irritant trilled a handful of his most famous songs were Piers Fucking Morgan and Jamie Fucking Redknapp.

A more motley crew of showbusiness menaces it is harder to imagine (presumably James Corden was ill or something).

WHERE ARE ISIS STORMTROOPERS WHEN YOU NEED THEM? WHERE ARE THEIR GUNBOATS AND THEIR TORPEDOES WHEN STING, MORGAN AND REDKNAPP ARE ONLY METRES AWAY FROM A WATERY HELL?

Drones

Fuck off, drones. Seriously, just fuck off. There's enough shit in the modern world without you adding to it and complicating things further. Little tiny planes that anyone can fly anywhere are just a technological development too far, and are just going to lead to too much fucking paperwork.

I'm all in favour of a bit of espionage now and again, but this drone thing is just bullshit. As a keen nude sunbather, I'm not going to feel comfortable getting my meat and two veg out in my back garden, in case some sneaky fucker flies a drone overhead equipped with a tiny camera.

Before I know it, pictures of my special are going to be all over Facebook and traded for bitcoins among erotic image collectors.

My tackle is my pride and joy, and a world in which I can't unleash it in private during the height of summer is a world that I don't think I want to live in.

BRING YOUR DRONES NEAR ME AND I WILL SHOOT THEM DOWN, STUFF THEM IN A SACK AND CHUCK THEM IN THE FUCKING SEA.

A printed version of Wikipedia

PediaPress sounds like a fucking dodgy name to give your company, but thankfully they're not about printing pamphlets for nonces – mind you, what they've really been up to is only slightly less heinous.

It's a crowdfunded venture, as most idiotic ideas are – the arena of the crowdfund is where the truly desperate go once they've run out of doors to have slammed in their face but still haven't got the fucking hint.

The big idea from PediaPress was to produce a printed version of the whole Wikipedia. I wish I was making this up, but no, they wanted to put all 2.6 billion words into a 1,000-volume book and take it on a tour of the world.

If that in itself isn't a bad enough idea, just think about how Wikipedia is constantly changing, being updated by users every second of every day. Their book would have been defunct as soon as they started printing it.

Needless to say, they didn't reach their crowdfunding target.

YOU'D BE BETTER OFF EXHIBITING A SNOOKER BALL THAT HAD BEEN UP A HORSE'S ARSE, AND IT WOULD HAVE BEEN CHEAPER AS WELL. GET IN THE FUCKING SEA.

Charlotte Higgins' ruined yoga retreat

'George Osborne ruined my yoga retreat,' read the headline of a *Guardian* piece by Charlotte Higgins a while ago.

CHARLOTTE HIGGINS RUINED MY FUCKING LIFE WITH THAT HEADLINE. PUT HER IN THE FUCKING SEA

£13.5k John Lewis mattress

We all like a decent night's sleep, and if you skimp when it comes to buying a mattress, you're potentially exposing yourself to a future filled with agonizing back pain, insanity caused from a lack of quality kip and an early death when you run out into traffic to chase a giant butterfly that has kidnapped your children but you're only hallucinating because of chronic sleep deprivation.

So, think twice before you opt for the £49 mattress at KING OF BEDZZZZ next time.

What you mustn't do, though, is head for John Lewis and consider the £13,500 mattress that appeared on their website recently. You probably wouldn't be allowed to try it out in store anyway – it's probably covered by an alarm that's triggered by invisible lasers when unrecognized DNA strays within six feet of it.

What the fuck is even *in* a mattress that can cause it to cost £13.5k? The only thing I can think that might be stuffed in it is £13k in used notes.

DESTINATION SEA FOR EVERYONE INVOLVED IN THE PRODUCTION OF THIS FUCKER WHO DIDN'T PIPE UP WITH 'ARE WE *REALLY* CHARGING THIRTEEN AND A HALF GRAND FOR THIS? SERIOUSLY?' YOUR COLLECTIVE NEGLECT FOR YOUR FELLOW HUMANS HAS

EARNED YOU A PLACE AMONG THE
FISHES.

Supermarket checkouts

Not the self-service ones – there's nothing particularly
wrong with those. Okay, so they might not always read
your barcodes and that whole 'unidentified object in the
bagging area' shit is a bit irksome, but look at the bigger
picture here – *no human interaction*.

No small talk with the cashier, who's also giving you
the stink-eye because you're a grown man buying an
industrial-sized bottle of Johnson's Baby Oil (I have a
skin condition! And needs!). No standing around waiting for the dozy fucker in front to realize that he's picked
up a leaking bottle of washing-up liquid and for the
whole checkout to be wiped.

No agitation caused by the twat behind you not using
the 'next customer please' bar and the creeping rage as
their shopping encroaches into your personal space,
leading you to reach for a bar and pointedly put it
between your shopping and theirs, while sighing huffily.
You're wasting your fucking breath – these pricks will
never learn!

Stick to the self-service checkout – just you and the
machine, it's the closest you'll ever get to retail nirvana.

PEOPLE IN SUPERMARKETS = ARSE-
HOLES. GET IN THE FUCKING SEA.

Stupid celebrity baby names

Celebrities are essentially fucking idiots. Their lives have been altered beyond all reasonable imagination because they're a bit talented at singing or dancing or acting or because they managed to do eight weeks in the Big Brother house without biting the ear off of one of their housemates. I imagine it's harder than it looks – I'd probably be carted out of there with some lobe stuck in my teeth in under three days.

Fame and adulation clearly rots the brain, though, because when they get around to breeding, and more specifically naming their children, all rational thought seems to vanish into thin air.

Would *you* fancy growing up saddled with the name Moxie CrimeFighter, just as the daughter of magician Penn Jillette must? Or being George Jr, George III, George IV, George V, George VI – the sons (or perhaps there's a daughter chucked in there as well) of former boxer George Foreman?

How about Audio Science, the son of minor comedy actor Shannyn Sossamon? Or Jamie Oliver's kids – Poppy Honey Rosie, Daisy Boo Pamela, Petal Blossom Rainbow and Buddy Bear Maurice. Hi gang!

Then there's Helen Baxendale's brood – Nell Marmalade, Eric Mustard and Vincent Mash. No, really.

Let's all tilt our heads sideways and give a sympathetic look at Bronx Mowgli Wentz, followed by a hard stare at his idiot parents, Ashlee Simpson and Pete Wentz. Or ruffle the hair of Jason Lee's kid, who he inexplicably named Pilot Inspektor, and tell him it'll be okay and he can change it by deed poll to something normal like Roy or Trevor when he's a bit older.

The most recent offender is former *Hollyoaks* actor and low-level media irritant Paul Danan, who has sired a son saddled with the name DeNiro. The fucking state of it – an actor of his standard naming his kid after one of the greatest in the business. It's like Olly Murs calling his kid Sinatra.

Shit. Olly Murs might breed one day. I've only just considered that. Fucking hell.

IT'S BAD ENOUGH THAT YOUR CHILDREN WILL BE DAMAGED FROM GROWING UP BEING REMINDED THAT THEIR MUM OR DAD ARE 'THAT WANKER FROM THE FILMS' WITHOUT SADDLING THEM WITH THE KIND OF NAME THAT WILL PRO-VOKE HOOTS OF DERISION FROM EVERY SINGLE MAN, WOMAN AND CHILD WHICH THEY COME ACROSS UNTIL THE DAY THEY DIE. GET IN THE FUCKING SEA.

The tip

Going to your local municipal dump is hard these days. If you're slightly illiterate or colour blind, you're fucked, and your best bet is to just drop everything in the general waste skip. But put it all in black bin liners, though, because if you get caught doing that by the bin Nazis that run things down there, you're double fucked.

Dumping laminate flooring? You'd better check and see if you can leave it in the wood skip. Who knows, it might class as garden waste if it's a dark enough brown – you can pretend it's a piece of tree. Does that old monitor work? Even if it doesn't you have to leave it in the designated area and don't lay it on its side or it might explode or release tuberculosis into the atmosphere.

Mate. Mate! That's the wrong kind of plastic – it's got screws in it. Take them out first and come back between 9 a.m. and 11 a.m. on Thursday, when the plastic-sifting team are here.

You can't come in with a van. Sorry, but a Citroën Berlingo counts as a van. It's in the rules – no, I haven't got a copy here but you can read them down at the town hall.

What's in those bags, mate? Couple of dead dogs? Yeah, just put them in general waste.

WHY CAN'T WE JUST DUMP EVERYTHING WE DON'T NEED IN ONE MASSIVE SKIP, SET THE CONTENTS ALIGHT WHEN IT'S FULL AND THEN TIP THE ASHES INTO THE FUCKING SEA? IT'S PROBABLY AS ENVIRONMENTALLY SOUND AS EIGHT DIFFERENT SKIPS. PROBABLY.

Twee marketing

Will the meek inherit the earth? Or maybe it'll be the geeks? Who knows, but we all need to remain vigilant and make sure that it isn't the twee that inherit it, because then we'll all be fucked.

Hopefully, due to the aforementioned tweeness, they won't have the gumption to enforce a total cultural take-over, but their passive-aggressive campaign via product marketing is becoming a bit too insidious to completely ignore.

Innocent and their bastard smoothies pioneered the modern-day tweevertising cult. On one of their cartons, they list its ingredients (with cutesy pictures, obviously) and at the end of the list, after bananas, blueberries and oranges, they tell us that the smoothie contains, 'o bunga-lows'. Ha! Because you don't put a bungalow in a smoothie! That would be BONKERS! And deeply illegal.

When that sort of vapid shite became inexplicably popular, the bandwagon began to gather pace, with the toilets on board Virgin Trains nabbing themselves a piece of this wacky action.

'Please don't flush nappies, sanitary towels, paper towels, gum, old phones, unpaid bills, junk mail, your ex's sweater, hopes, dreams or goldfish down this toilet,' reads the sign, which can only serve to enrage you while you're having a dump just outside Retford.

Also guilty of this overfriendly fuckery is Malmai-son – before you can open the wrapped bar of soap in one of their bathrooms, you have to look at a label that reads, 'Getting jiggy wit da figgy – where your hands bin, we can tell from that grin. You've been committing the 5th deadly sin. In cases of lust, this soap is a must. Whadda ya mean, you can't be fussed?'

What? Are they accusing me of monking one out in the bed while watching Susanna Reid on *Good Morning Britain*? Wow – turns out they know me quite well . . .

STOP TRYING TO BE OUR CRAZY CHUMS AND JUST DO YOUR FUCKING JOB AS PRODUCTS. TASTE NICE, CLEAN OUR HANDS AND FLUSH AWAY OUR TURDS WITHOUT CAUSING OUR GENITALS TO SHRINK UP INTO OUR BODIES FROM YOUR CLOYING AWFULNESS. THIS MARKETING WANK BELONGS IN THE FUCKING SEA.

The Matisse outrage

Britain's Got Talent is an awful, awful cultural phenomenon, rewarding grinding. mediocrity with a fleeting glimpse of fame. If you can name more than four past winners of *BGT*, you're a massive part of the problem and you should already be in the fucking sea.

Perhaps the lowest point in the show's woeful history came in 2015, when a dog act scooped the top prize. A stunt border collie named Matisse (I looked it up, right?) was the public's choice, but afterwards there was an almighty furore when it emerged that a second, similar-looking dog (named Chase) had appeared during the final, walking across a tightrope.

Did Britain vote en masse for Matisse believing that he was the dog on the tightrope? Should Chase have worn a T-shirt with his name on it so that we knew we were looking at a different dog? How the fuck is this even a thing that led to so much controversy?

If you voted for Matisse and then felt duped because there was a second stunt dog, *are you even aware of how these fucking talent shows operate, you dolt*? You're being manipulated at every turn, voting for acts that have been handpicked so that you'll let them into your hearts and hand over your voting coins so that Cowell can boost his cash reserves and stock up on low-necked T-shirts and fucking Ray-Bans.

At least you didn't vote for the other dog – the ventriloquist one with the false face that looked like its heart was about to explode. At least you didn't fuck *that* decision up.

I'll leave the last word to Jules O'Dwyer, the 'brains' behind Matisse and Chase and the rest of the act. She said afterwards: 'Who is feeling cheated by it? They don't understand the concept of a live show.' Which, to me, translates as 'fuck 'em'.

AGITATED BECAUSE YOU GOT CONFUSED BY TWO SIMILAR DOGS ON A TV SHOW AND NOW YOU WANT YOUR 50P BACK? IT'S IN THE FUCKING SEA – GO AND LOOK FOR IT.

Margaret Thatcher porn

It takes some serious work to make pornography unpalatable, but knocking together a rhythm film based on the life and times of Margaret Thatcher might be as good a way as any of stopping any growth in the genitalia sector.

That's exactly what late-night satellite channel Television X did not so long ago – called *The Iron Lady Garden*, it retold the career of the woman who fucked entire communities in the 1980s, portraying her as a sex-obsessed woman who enjoyed fucking her advisors, cabinet ministers and other assorted dignitaries as well.

Well, I assume that's what happens – I've only seen the trailer on YouTube and it's a bit tame for obvious reasons. In fact, I've got a sudden urge to go and watch it again now. And again . . . and again . . .

GET IN THE FUCKING SEA YOU SEXY, EVIL, CONFUSING, SEXY, DEAD WITCH.

iTunes

Fact – no one in Britain with an Apple device is listening to any music on it that was created after 2011. That's because they're all scared witless of fucking iTunes. Make a single wrong move while trying to sync your iPhone with your laptop and there's a strong chance you'll lose all of your music, your screen display will turn itself sideways, and you'll somehow install a program that reads out all of your emails, web pages and documents to you in the voice of Noel Edmonds.

Over the years, Apple has transformed iTunes from a simple way of making your music portable into a bloated, labyrinthine piece of shit that is so complicated that it'll drive you into a state of such high irritation where hearing *any* music at all will shred your nerves and cause you to self-harm.

You genuinely wouldn't be surprised if the next version of iTunes sprouted tentacles and burst out of your monitor, grabbing you by the throat and choking you to death.

WE JUST WANT TO HEAR OUR LADY GAGA ALBUMS – WE DON'T WANT TO BE SUCKED INTO SOME KIND OF HARROW-ING REMAKE OF THE FUCKING *MATRIX*. SORT IT OUT OR GET IN THE FUCKING SEA.

Door knocker/cold caller companies – and idiots who buy from them

'Good morning, sir – are you happy with your current gas and electricity supplier? It's just that the company I represent, Acme Utilities, are in the area today and offer-ing what we think is a fantastic deal which I'd just like to tell you a little bit about without allowing you to get a single fucking word in edgeways.

'Just sign up today and I'll add a 15 per cent discount off your first monthly direct debit payment from one of the nine tariffs that I'll explain to you in such haste that you won't know whether you're coming or going. You'll be tied into your new price plan for three years, which sounds like a good thing apart from the stuff in the small print that will see your bills fly through the roof once winter comes. And the last thing you need in winter is no fucking roof.

'I can see that you're becoming increasingly bemused by all of this so I'll just get you to sign on the dotted line while you're at your most vulnerable and itching to get back to *Deal Or No Deal*. There's a sign-up charge that I haven't mentioned and the slight possibility that your gas and electricity will be temporarily disconnected for three days while your account is switched over from your current supplier.

'They'll probably be whacking you with an early exit fee as well, and this brief one-sided conversation will end up costing you an extra £450 over the next year, while earning me £7.95 in commission. Goodbye, and enjoy the subsequent pain that this encounter will undoubtedly cause you, you fucking mug.'

YOUR SCABROUS KNOCKING WILL GO UNHEARD WHEN IT IS ON THE DOORS OF WRECKED SHIPS THAT ARE LYING AT THE BOTTOM OF THE OCEAN, YOU SCAMMING FUCKING WEASELS.

Pick Up Girls smartwatch

A crowdfunded piece of utter shitfuckery, dreamed up by the kind of angry loner who can't get girls to talk to him because he's an angry loner, this supposedly spunks confidence into your brain by subliminal messages and hypnosis, turning you from a seething loser into a winning lothario.

Yeah, right, course it fucking does. If it ever catches on, it'll simply broadcast the message that women should give you a swerve because you're a desperate pick-up artist who doesn't even have enough charisma or imagination to do the job without hypnotizing yourself first. You hopeless wanger.

THE BEST THING ABOUT THIS PIECE OF SHITTY TECHNOLOGY IS THAT IT INSTANTLY MARKS OUT ITS WEARER AS THE KIND OF FUCKWEASEL THAT NEEDS TO BE AVOIDED AT ALL COSTS. INTO THE SEA HE GOES WITH IT.

Gif pronunciation

We all love gifs, don't we? Those short animated images that take too long to load on your laptop or don't even load at all on your phone, and they're always either not funny or a bit underwhelming. No, hang on, we fucking hate gifs.

Turns out that we're not even pronouncing 'gif' properly. The inventor of them, Steve Wilhite, reckons it should be pronounced 'jif' and not 'gif'. Seeing as how it's an acronym for Graphics Interchange Format, it's fair to say that Wilhite can take his pronunciation bullshit and jam it up his fucking a-hole.

Anyway, as any cleaning product fan knows, Jif was renamed Cif a few years ago, so I'll be calling his gifs cifs from now on. The cunt.

GET IN THE FUCKING SEA, WILHITE, YOU DERANGED PRONUNCIATION FASCIST.

Methinks cunts

It's not the sixteenth century – stop saying 'methinks' in your social media postings. As in: 'The working week is almost over – methinks a little alcoholic therapy is in order.'

Or if you do, kindly go the whole hog and start using 'forsooth' and 'verily' as well, you wankers.

OH, AND GO AND DIE FROM THE PLAGUE WHILE YOU'RE ABOUT IT – THAT OR PUT YOURSELF IN THE FUCKING SEA. EITHER WILL DO.

LinkedIn

Want to know where everyone you might ever want to avoid is? They're all on LinkedIn, the infernal business networking website. Joining in is easy enough – stick your CV and a selfie on there, 'connect' with some people you work with, and a world of big business possibilities is wide open to you.

A week later, you'll have remembered that you signed up, log in to see what's happened and will find out that three people have looked at your profile. No offers of work from FTSE-100 corporations and not even any ice bucket challenges like on Facebook.

You're not in the true LinkedIn loop and that's because you're not a grabbing, business-obsessed prick. If you were, you'd be hooking up with providers of training schemes and sellers of marketing strategy pamphlets and signing up for networking events that take place in a meeting room in a Premier Inn just off the M6 and which only seven people turn up for. One of them is Ray Parker Jr, and no one there, not even Ray himself, knows why.

You'll probably get more business done down the precinct, selling your nan's Temazepam to the scrotes that sit on the ground outside the kebab shop.

THERE'S A SEA-BASED VERSION OF LINKEDIN CALLED SINKEDIN, AND YOU ALL FUCKING BELONG IN IT.

King Lear *performed by sheep*

Sadly, this was exactly what it claims to be – a production of one of Shakespeare's finest works, but with woolly farm beasts instead of actors. And only £10 a ticket for the thirty-minute production, which was staged in London's cunt-addled Hoxton (fucking obviously) in the summer of 2015.

'Are you still going ahead with that *King Lear* sheep thing?'

'Yes, of course.'

'You sure about that?'

'Yes! It's going to be tremendous!'

'You've fucking lost it, mate.'

IS THERE ROOM IN THE SEA FOR THE BELL END WHO CAME UP WITH THIS AS WELL AS THE ARSEHOLES WHO PAID GOOD MONEY TO WATCH IT? OF COURSE THERE IS!

'Inspirational' Tube station signs

Have you seen them? Those handwritten signs that appear in the ticket halls of certain stations on the London Underground? Sometimes they'll show a pithy piece of 'life advice' or a notable quotation that relates to something topical. The idea is to make you stop for a moment amid all the hustle and bustle and reflect for a short while as you consider the poignant words of Chaucer, Larkin or Coldplay.

FUCK OFF – HAVE YOU BEEN ON THE TUBE DURING RUSH HOUR? THE ONLY THING YOU FIND YOURSELF REFLECTING ON IS WHY THERE'S SO MANY FUCKING IDIOTS GETTING IN YOUR FUCKING WAY AND HOW YOU CAN GET THE FUCKERS TO MOVE. JUST WRITE 'STOP DAWDLING, YOU CUNTS!' ON ALL THE SIGNS SO THAT NO ONE IS WANDERING AROUND LOST IN A WORLD OF QUOTES AND POETRY WHEN THEY SHOULD BE IN THE FUCKING SEA INSTEAD.

3D printing

Be careful what you wish for, everyone. Oh, it's easy to get excited about being able to 3D print bicycle parts and false limbs and service station cutlery and all that, but it's the thin end of the wedge.

I read somewhere that you can 3D print out all the working parts of a gun and then put them together. And bullets too, obviously. Then what? You'll be able to print out fucking Nazis and before you know it we'll be swarmed by the Fourth Reich.

How do you know that Hitler didn't exist in the future and just travelled back from 2070, stopping off at 2012 to bring us 3D printing in order to set the trap for future Nazi rule? Obviously he then whizzed back to the 1920s and did the whole World War 2 thing as a massive decoy.

We're sleepwalking into a future of death and destruction, masterminded by an invincible 3D printed version of Hitler that he did himself before sacrificing himself in 1945.

Fucking obvious when you think about it.

THIS VOODOO PRINTING BULLSHIT NEEDS DROPPING IN THE FUCKING SEA BEFORE IT DESTROYS THE HUMAN RACE THAT WE KNOW AND DESPISE.

Twitter eggs

Quick tip for Twitter novices – if you want to work out who to avoid like the plague on the globally renowned social media website, there's a surefire way of spotting the cranks and head-the-balls. They're the ones who have Twitter's default 'white egg on a coloured background' as their avatar.

Think about it – in order to put your personal stamp on your Twitter account, all you have to do is click on the profile edit section and upload a picture – *any* picture – to your account. Simple. Done.

Not these fuckers, though – not the eggs. They're either too busy spraying their rabid opinions out in a scattergun series of deranged tweets or they just don't have the technical skill to upload an image.

You'll find them PREDOMINANTLY TWEETING IN UPPER CASE, focusing their weirdness and/or rage on A-list celebrities who will never reply to them in a million years or just barging into conversations between two people who don't know them and haven't asked for their input.

Outside of Twitter, the egg is supposed to represent new life – within Twitter, it signifies lunacy and danger.

WHAT KIND OF SOCIETAL THREAT WOULD SPEND THEIR TIME WRITING IN UPPER CASE? GET THEM IN THE FUCKING SEA.

Retweeting praise

Are you a celebrity who has just completed a piece of work that has been offered up for public consumption? Well done, clever clogs! Is your Twitter mentions column now starting to fill up with positive feedback from the thousands upon thousands of lickarses who follow you on the globally popular social media website?

Here's a thought – perhaps you could share that feedback with all of your followers by retweeting it. Every single piece of it. Go on, they all want to share in the joy as your ego swells to twice its usual size (even though it's pretty fucking massive to begin with).

That's right, keep it coming. More praise from strangers, broadcast to thousands. It doesn't make you look like some kind of arrogant yet exceedingly needy prick at all. Keep it coming!

OR, JUST GET IN THE FUCKING SEA.

Thatcher's wardrobe

Hats off to the geniuses at London's Victoria and Albert Museum, who, when offered the opportunity to exhibit the clothes formerly belonging to the late, hated Margaret Thatcher, declined while throwing some major shade with their response.

The V&A said: 'The museum is responsible for chronicling fashionable dress, and its collecting policy tends to focus on acquiring examples of outstanding aesthetic or technical quality.'

In other words, while she was clearly deranged, the despised tyrant dressed like a miffed widow, and we've got no desire to try and persuade anyone to come and look at her skirts in their fifty shades of dark blue. Thank you but fuck off.

THATCHER'S CLOTHES BELONG IN THE FUCKING SEA, ALONG WITH HER IDEAS AND HER FUCKING WIG.

People who buy followers on Twitter

Have *you* done this? You do realize it's fucking obvious to everyone else, right? That's because there's no way that your Twitter feed, filled as it is with replies to that bloke from *Pointless*, retweets of competitions where you could win £50 worth of Muscletech Platinum Creatine but won't and a photo of the dashboard of your car that you tweeted by accident but don't know how to delete, could ever hope to muster 17,000 followers.

You've bought them for £45, and they've all got computer-generated names and avatars, and the whole sorry saga has made you look like the epic dick that you surely are.

THE ONLY TRUE FRIENDS YOU ARE EVER LIKELY TO HAVE ARE TINY FISH THAT SWIM AROUND YOUR ANKLES AS YOU STRUGGLE TO RETURN TO THE SURFACE OF THE FUCKING SEA.

Baby bling

Your baby does not need to be dressed from head to toe in diamond-encrusted romper suits. Your baby just needs your time and love and attention. Your baby does not need to wear designer labels because it will grow out of the clothes in about forty minutes and anyway it'll be sick all down them and they'll start to stink and they'll shrink when you boil wash them (the clothes, not the baby).

Your baby *definitely* does not need to wear high-heel baby shoes from peeweepumps.com, and anyone who indulges in this ridiculous behaviour needs to be closely watched by a child protection agency.

YOUR BABY NEEDS TO BE PLACED INTO THE CARE OF A RESPONSIBLE ADULT FIGURE, AND YOU NEED TO GET IN THE FUCKING SEA.

The London garden bridge

It's almost like something from a cheese-fuelled dream. Joanna Lumley, yearning for a new bridge to be built over the Thames, but not just any old bridge. No, this is a *garden bridge*, filled with trees and flowers and probably worms and ants and wasps as well.

The bridge is something that Ms Lumley has hankered after for years now, and it was originally planned to be funded privately. Fair enough, I mean we all have dreams – mine is to persuade the people at Laughing Cow to start selling cheese triangles with five dry-roasted peanuts stuffed in them (if you haven't tried this, you're truly missing out).

Then things started to get murkier. Transport for London became a backer of the bridge project, offering to pledge £30 million to it (later cut to £10 million). Transport for London, of course, isn't a private company, but there's no second-guessing when it comes to Boris Johnson and what he might do as mayor of the capital.

After all, he delivered a cable car across the Thames that hardly anyone uses and that only hoovered up a massive chunk of public money, so you've got to believe in him.

And even though the bridge will be closed to the public on a regular basis for private functions, that shouldn't be a concern to anyone – just imagine that the TfL money is subsidizing the times when it's open to one and all.

The fact that Joanna Lumley has known Boris Johnson since he was four years of age is irrelevant here, so don't start thinking otherwise. The notion that when Johnson was probably hitting his wanking stride at the age of fourteen, Joanna was thirty-two and was being regularly photographed in various states of undress on tropical beaches for magazine features is also meaningless here – she's just as entitled to pitch for a garden bridge across the Thames as the rest of us.

Do *you* want a garden bridge? There's loads of bridgeless bits of the Thames left, so why not drop Boris Johnson or his mayoral successor an email. Me, I'll stick to dreams of cheese with nuts in it.

YOU KNOW WHERE YOUR FUCKING BRIDGE WOULD LOOK REALLY GOOD? YEP...

Apprentice *losers going rogue*

That feeling of having been booted off of Lord Sir Alan Sugar's big business 'process' (game show) must be liberating. Just imagine the career possibilities that lie before you now that you've proved yourself to be among the most talented entrepreneurs of the year.

I don't mean business opportunities, but the chance to make a complete tool of yourself on low-grade reality TV (obviously, Katie Hopkins is a special case and is covered elsewhere in this book).

Once they've been sacked by the man with a face like a lion trying to escape from inside a giant testicle, the gobbiest of them inevitably crop up on various, lesser reality shows, the trickle-down effect of shit British telly in all its glory.

Finish second or third on *The Apprentice* and you might well bag ten days or so in the *Celebrity Big Brother* house, with a sizey cheque at the end of it all and a lifelong memory of being kept awake by the flatulence of a former boy band member.

Finish between fourth and sixth and you can be sure of a couple of appearances on some kind of Sky One karaoke/gymnastics/both at the same time shit parade. Anything lower than sixth, and a new showbiz career isn't looking so promising – you'll get nothing better than a non-broadcast pilot for Channel 5, in which you live in an abandoned hospital with seventeen orangutans for a week.

Could be worse, though – you could have won *The Apprentice* and found yourself having to work with Lord Sir Alan Sugar.

GET OFF OUR SCREENS AND GET IN THE FUCKING SEA.

Unboxing videos

Undeniable proof that there's something for everyone on the internet, the popularity of unboxing videos, where people film themselves opening up brand-new products is as baffling as it is chilling.

To the outsider, it can look like some kind of porn substitute for people whose genitalia have long since grown over with moss but there's an audience for it, and some of the top unboxers are making a living from You-Tube ad revenue as millions of people log on and watch them open their shopping.

Everything from gadgets to clothes to perfume to children's toys feature in these videos, and if you're not careful, you can easily lose a few days to gawping at them in fear and disbelief.

Trust me, you've never known true horror until you've seen a YouTube video of a grown man filming himself opening umpteen packets of Match Attax football cards and wrongly pronouncing the names of half the players. And he's making money from it, enabling him to buy even more shit that he can mispronounce.

THESE PERVERTS NEED BOXING UP AND DROPPING OFF A CLIFF INTO THE FUCK-ING SEA.

Earth's Fifty Worst Humans:
The Top Ten

10 Toby Young

Imagine a giant white chocolate Malteser with a face and a pair of glasses drawn on it, exhaling a load of wind in the shape of words, smug opinions and sneery shite. That's Toby Young for you.

Seemingly balding from a very early age (always a trigger for someone to turn out as a complete prick), Young has been letting his mouth go over the past few years on the subject of free schools, acting almost as an unofficial spokesman for them for the government and their rabid obsession with allowing them to thrive. In fact, he has even co-founded one himself.

Unfortunately, while he is certainly intelligent, Young is utterly bereft of charm, and listening to him wanging out his unwelcome thoughts is about as pleasurable as picking bubble gum out of your hair with a tuning fork (a pastime that Young himself will never be troubled by).

Arguably the best thing Young ever did was to tweet a picture of himself with a minor head injury after he was knocked off his bike by a passing car. No one is suggesting it was a deliberate act, okay?

GET IN THE FUCKING SEA, YOU NON-SENSICAL OPINIONS GIMP.

9 Commander Hadfield

Is it wrong to think ill of a man who enjoyed a thirty-five-year career as a military pilot and astronaut, later becoming the first Canadian to walk in space? No – no it is fucking not.

Hadfield shot to fame when he posted his cover version of David Bowie's 'Space Oddity' on YouTube in 2013, filmed during one of his stints on the International Space Station. It turned him into an overnight star, with 25 million views of the video.

Couple of things here: one, as cover versions of Bowie songs go, it was pretty woeful. Hadfield has a thin, reedy voice and he sounds more like a depressed cleric than a go-getting astronaut. Two, what the fuck is he doing pissing about on the ISS karaoke machine when there's valuable work to be done instead? He should be spending his time looking for UFO attacks and dodging meteorites instead of playing out his little singing astronaut wank fantasy.

What would have happened if Earth had been invaded by an alien fleet while he was out the back, trilling into a microphone? Did he only do one song? Is he going back up on to the ISS to do an album? Who the fuck is paying for all of this frippery?

GET BACK DOWN ON TO PLANET EARTH, HADFIELD, AND TAKE YOUR RIGHTFUL PLACE IN THE FUCKING SEA, YOU SKIVING LITTLE SPACE CUNT.

8 Paul Hollywood

'Awwww, Paul Hollywood? How the fuck can you hate Paul Hollywood? He's got the blue eyes and he can bake, and what else does a modern man need in his locker?' Fuck off. You're not looking at the full picture. Forget about the eyes and the fresh bread, we're not trying to sell a house here.

One. He jams his hands in the front pockets of his overly snug jeans while he's talking to people.

Two. He's slightly too fond of being photographed by national publications while dressed head to toe in biking leathers and giving it a bit too much smoulder with the aforementioned eyes.

Three. He owns a car that has a special crystal instead of an ignition key.

Four. He's far more wealthy, successful and popular than me.

Five. Fuck off.

GET YOUR HANDS OUT OF YOUR FUCKING POCKETS AND GET IN THE FUCKING SEA, YOU TRAGIC, WANDERING MID-LIFE CRISIS

7 Ultra Romance

Wacky name, deeply annoying guy – he works for half the year and takes the other six months off to live on a shoestring and travel around the world on his bike. A true child of the earth, Ultra has a bank account but only uses it for buying and selling bike parts on eBay. The rest of his cash is buried in little bags in places where only he knows it is.

He sounds great, but if you go online and look up pictures of him, riding around in the snow with his shirt off and posing for photos with one foot up on his bike wheel, you'll quickly come to the conclusion that he's a self-absorbed knobhead.

FUCK YOU, 'ULTRA' – I'VE DUG UP ALL YOUR MONEY AND CHUCKED IT IN THE FUCKING SEA. HOPEFULLY THE TAX PEOPLE WILL COME AFTER YOU WHILE YOU'RE IN THERE LOOKING FOR IT AND JAMMING IT DOWN YOUR TOO-TIGHT SPEEDOS, YOU TWAT.

6 George Osborne

Hard to know where to start with this treacher-ous little shitheel – there's the fact that his UK financial recovery is founded on borrowing even more money than ever before but persuading everyone to look at the deficit figure instead. There's the fact that most of his budgetary schemes have missed their targets and the 'recovery' that he trumpets about barely even exists.

There's that fucking face and voice and plastic hairstyle and that gurning he sometimes does during Prime Minister's Questions on a Wednesday that make you wonder why he doesn't have an early night on a Tuesday. There's the fact that he's a key part of arguably the most vicious government of all time – one that seems to actively despise large parts of the population that it's supposed to be looking after.

There's the fact that the National Trust forked out £375k to fix his lavish country retreat at Dorneywood (that's equal to almost 100 years of Jobseeker's Allowance at £73.10 per week). Or his naked ambition to become the next Prime Minister even though he's the sort of bloke that you'd spill your drink over and run away from if he sat next to you and talked to you in a pub.

He's a fucking atrocity and he needs to be stopped.

GET HIM IN THE FUCKING SEA BEFORE HIS EVIL SCHEME TO BECOME PRIME MINISTER COMES TO FRUITION, AND THE POOR AND NEEDY CRUMBLE TO DUST AS A RESULT OF HIS EVIL FUCKING DOINGS.

5 Banksy

Wanksy more like.

GET IN THE FUCKING SEA, WITH YOUR
BACKWARDS-BASEBALL-CAP-WEARING
FUCKSMUGGERY, YOUR TEENAGE-LEVEL
SOCIAL COMMENT, YOUR RIDICULOUS
IDENTITY MASKING AND YOUR SHITTY
PICTURES.

4 Iain Duncan Smith

Iain Duncan Smith (IDS) should not be confused with
Irritable Bowel Syndrome (IBS). The two diseases are
in no way linked, and anyway Iain Duncan Smith isn't
even a disease, and who said he was?

No, he's actually a cunt of biblical proportions.
Currently the Secretary of State for Work and Pensions,
his recent activities make his spell as leader of
the Conservative Party between 2001 and 2003 look
like a free roller disco run by Mother Teresa by
comparison.

Back then, he was a slightly weird, bald knobhead
who freaked the nation out by saying, 'The quiet man is
here to stay . . . and he's TURNING UP THE VOL-
UME,' at the Tory Party conference – a piece of footage

that is guaranteed to get naughty children running to their bedrooms in fear.

So woeful was his spell as party leader that he ended up calling for his critics to put forward a vote of confidence in him or shut up. The vote of no confidence was duly delivered and he was replaced by the even creepier Michael Howard.

It's impossible to say whether all of this had been brewing in his mind when he became boss of the DWP, but he's attacked the job with the vigour of a police dog on a burglar's leg, gleefully stripping away benefits across the board and introducing fitness for work tests for the severely ill and disabled that in many cases have found that they're fine for work actually and that they should knuckle down and get on with it.

Go on – get out of those leg irons and find yourself a zero-hours job in the Sports Direct warehouse. Who knows – perhaps your smashed legs will get better once you're using them a bit more often, yes?

After all – what doesn't kill you can only make you stronger. Unless it fucking kills you, that is.

THEY'LL BE TESTING YOU TO SEE IF YOU'RE FIT FOR THE FUCKING SEA ONCE YOU'VE BEEN CONDEMNED TO ITS HORRIBLE CURRENTS, YOU VILE PIECE OF SHIT.

3 *Jeremy Clarkson*

Jeremy Clarkson is for men who reckon they 'tell it like it is' but in fact repeatedly tell it like it isn't and like it must never be allowed to be ever again. Jeremy Clarkson is for men who are weirdly proud of their moobs. Jeremy Clarkson is for men who say, 'I'd give it ten minutes if I were you.' Jeremy Clarkson is for men who aren't keen on that bloke who's taken over the off-licence. Jeremy Clarkson is for men who reckon they could turn this country around if they were given six months to run it. Jeremy Clarkson is for men who are certain that there's been no great music made since 1979 apart from that one by Kings of Leon. Jeremy Clarkson is for men who call their tiny shed their 'man cave'. Jeremy Clarkson is for men who die of cancer because they ignored the warning signs. Jeremy Clarkson is for men who are convinced that Jeremy Corbyn is a Russian secret agent. Jeremy Clarkson is for men who drink four pints on a Friday night and then drive three miles home because they know what they're doing. Jeremy Clarkson is for men who secretly want to fuck their niece. Jeremy Clarkson is for men who never, ever want to see a black James Bond. Jeremy Clarkson is one of Earth's worst humans.

JEREMY CLARKSON IS FOR MEN WHO BELONG IN THE FUCKING SEA.

It takes a special skill to stand out among the other contenders for the title of Earth's Worst Human, but Hopkins seems to be almost on a mission to make it her life's achievement.

There are hordes of rude, ignorant objectionable shitehawks everywhere we look these days, but Hopkins has condensed the very worst of human nature and used it to transform herself into the ultimate fairy godmother of bile, spite and hatred.

The sight and sound of this shrill, patronizing, rent-a-gob is the one thing that is always guaranteed to send my mouth lurching towards my own elbows in a deranged attempt to chew them off, fuelled by embarrassment, disgust and rage.

It's hard to think of a minority group that she hasn't turned against ever since she failed to win Lord Sir Alan Sugar's business idiots' contest. Fat people, the unemployed, tattooed celebrities, mothers who take more than three weeks' maternity leave and even some of her kids' friends have all had it in the neck from her.

Like a junkie forever chasing that first sweet hit, she has become increasingly rabid of late, going in harder and stronger on targets that surely deserve only sympathy.

Describing refugees as 'cockroaches', she wrote in her *Sun* column: 'No, I don't care. Show me pictures of coffins, show me bodies floating in water, play violins and show me skinny people looking sad. I still don't care. Because in the next minute you'll show me pictures of aggressive young men at Calais, spreading like norovirus on a cruise ship.'

Then of course, hundreds and hundreds of people actually did start dying, their corpses floating in the water and she was made to look like a complete shithouse. Small comfort.

IN THE FUCKING SEA YOU GO, COCKROACH – THERE'LL BE A GUNSHIP DEPLOYED ON THE WATER JUST IN CASE YOU TRY TO RESURFACE. YOU KNOW, JUST LIKE THE ONE YOU ASKED FOR, YOU FUCKER.

1 David Cameron

Number one. Pig-fucking little cunt.

GET IN THE FUCKING SEA.